To Michaela

Provenance

A Legacy of Immigrants

by

Roberta Watson Richardson

Thanks for your help!

Roberta

Provenance

A Legacy of Immigrants

by

Roberta Watson Richardson

All rights reserved. This book is protected under the copyright laws of the United States of America. No part of this publication may be reproduced, stored in a retrieval system or transmitted in any form or by an means, electronic, mechanical, photocopying, recording or otherwise, with the written permission of the author.

ISBN: 978-1717598387

Contents

Introduction

Origins (listing) 1
    Watson Immigrant Ancestors 1
    Walker Immigrant Ancestors 4

Virginians 5
    Earliest Arrivals 8
        Francis and Agnes Barrett 8
        Capt. Raleigh Croshaw and Katherine Croshaw 10
        John Davis 12
        John English 13
        Capt. Thomas Graves 14
        Samuel Matthew 17
        William and Thomas Powell 19

    The "Second Sons" 23
        William and Robert Black 23
        William and Mary Bostick 26
        Giles Carter 28
        Thomas and William Peter Christian 31
        John Coffey 37
        Robert Coleman 40
        James Crewes 56
        Elizabeth Gorusch/Gorsuch 59
        Capt. Henry Isham 62
        William Leake 63
        Thomas Mask 65
        Helen Metland/Maitland 67
        Richard New 69
        Colonel William Randolph 72
        Joseph and John "Rocky Creek" Watson 79
        The Webbs: Alexander, William, John Richard, John 82

Refugees 87
    German: Johan Jurg and Johan Michael Meisser 87

Scot-Irish: Thomas Wallace 91
French Huguenots: Peter Tuly and Anthony Toncray 96
Quakers: Harlan, Buffington, Francis, Duck, Oborn and
    Cooke 104
California Swiss: Frank X. Walker 109
Cherokees 114
    Amatoya Moytoy 114
    Nancy "Nan'yehi" Ward 115
    Moses "Tu-Lu-Squit" Parris 117
Bibliography 121

Provenance: A Legacy of Immigrants

Provenance means the origin or source of something. Usually that something is a valuable piece of art or antique, but humans also have origins and sources. I've been seeking our family origins for a very long time and provenance is the best word I can find to define what I have been looking for. This book identifies 90 immigrants and, for as many as I could trace, their provenance before they crossed the Atlantic and their roles in creating the America we enjoy today. Their provenance is a legacy to those who have descended from them.

Introduction

It's one of my favorite memories. We're together on Calton Hill—my children, grandchildren and me—overlooking the rooftops of Edinburgh, Scotland, and Edinburgh Castle in the distance.

We're nearing the end of an extraordinary journey in one of the places our ancestors had tread for thousands of years. Edinburgh was inhabited by cave dwellers 10,000 years ago, by ancient tribes of Votadinis, Brittonics, Gododdins and Angles, and by Roman soldiers as their empire spread into Scotland in the first century CE.

A favorite memory of our British Isles journey is the view of Edinburg and Edinburg Castle from Calton Hill.

In June of 2016, we were visiting the British Isles to explore the sources of our early family history. Especially in Edinburgh, almost everywhere we turned we could feel the presence of our early ancestors.

King David I, an early cousin, founded Edinburgh in the 12th century. When he built Edinburgh Castle, he included a memorial chapel to another cousin, his mother, the sainted Queen Margaret, wife of King Malcolm III. King Robert de Bruce, my 21st great-grandfather, captured and destroyed most of the castle buildings in 1314, except for Saint Margaret's chapel

At the entrance of Edinburgh Castle, a statue of King Robert stands next to William Wallace, the martyred hero of our family's Wallace Clan. A stained glass window depicts Queen Margaret and a statue of King David stands at St. Giles Kirk in Edinburgh. Ancestors of our Watson Clan were recorded in Edinburgh as early as the late 1300s, but they probably were there much earlier before people were identified by family names.

On either side of the entrance to Edinburgh Castle are statues of our ancestor, King Robert de Brus (right), and William Wallace, the martyred hero of our family's Wallace Clan.

Before we left for our two-week journey through England, Ireland, Scotland and a bit of France, I prepared a list of the ancestral names to look for and places connected with our history. It was compiled quickly and missed as much as it contained. After the trip, I decided to write this book to share with my family our exceptional heritage and to encourage others to search for their cultural heritage in the lands of their immigrant ancestors.

Most of our ancestors arrived in the Colony of Virginia, the first permanently settled English colony in North America. A few were members of the Virginia Company that formed the colony's first settlement in Jamestown during the early 1600s. Many were the so-called "second sons" of English nobility. In England, the law of primogeniture favored the first sons inheriting lands and titles. That left later sons to enter the military or the clergy, or to go to the colonies to make their fortune. Early Virginia evolved as a society descended from these members of the

English gentry who inherited land grants or land in Virginia. They formed part of what became the southern elite in America.

It is not difficult to trace the ancestries of wealthy immigrants to the American colonies. Their families are proud of their heritage and have gone to great lengths to record and share their links to early kings, queens and other nobility whose history was recorded by scribes and storytellers. For the most part, it is these histories I have been able to research and share in this book.

Of course, not all of our immigrant ancestors were wealthy and their stories are harder to research. It is estimated that at least one-half to two-thirds of immigrants who came to the American colonies were not of this elite class. Landowners needed cheap labor to work the land and care for their families. Because passage to the colonies was expensive, the Virginia Company developed the system of indentured servitude to attract workers. Servants typically worked four to seven years in exchange for passage, room, board, lodging and freedom dues. Their contract may have included at least 25 acres of land, a year's worth of corn, arms, a cow and new clothes. Some servants did rise to become part of the colonial elite, but for the majority, satisfaction was a modest life as a free man in a burgeoning colonial economy.

Other early immigrants came to escape religious persecution or seek religious freedom, including the Pilgrims, Puritans, French Huguenots and Quakers. Another major wave of immigration occurred from

A Scottish piper welcomes my family to Scotland.

around 1815 to 1865. While much of our recorded family history dates back to colonial America, a few of our immigrant ancestors were part of these later migrations.

In the 1840s, almost half of America's immigrants were from Ireland, which had experienced a massive famine. Typically impoverished, these Irish immigrants settled near their point of arrival in cities along the East Coast. Between 1820 and 1930, some 4.5 million Irish migrated to the United States.

Also in the 19th century, the United States received some 5 million German immigrants. Many of them journeyed to the present-day Midwest to buy farms or congregated in such cities as Milwaukee, St. Louis and Cincinnati. In the national census of 2000, more Americans claimed German ancestry than any other group.

After years of research, I've identified most of our immigrant ancestors. Ninety of them are listed in the following chapter. Those I haven't found have names that are among the most common in America and Northern Europe: Watson, Smith, Miller and Hughes. I've included one of our Watson immigrants in this book, but there is another line, equally as important to our paternal Watson history, that I haven't been able to follow across the Atlantic. The Smiths, Millers and Hughes were among our maternal ancestors who gathered in California during the Gold Rush of 1849. People who made that journey often left their family histories behind, and there are too many with their surnames to depend on the sketchy public records of early America.

Early historical records tend to tell only the stories that the storytellers want to remember. Throughout history, heroes have been remembered but embarrassing episodes are swept under the rug. No matter how successful an ancestor might have been throughout most of his life, if he squanders the family fortune or ends his days in prison, he probably will be forgotten in family histories. I have always wanted to tell the whole story about my family, to scratch below the surface to piece together elements that some would rather avoid.

For example, I've learned that one of my great-grandfathers probably was a pirate. While some of his descendants chose to cover up that possibility (my grandmother told us he was a sea captain) I think it just adds flavor to our diverse ancestry.

It's distressing to realize that most of our early Virginia ancestors owned African slaves. Because slaves often took the surnames of their former owners, I have to accept that African Americans whose surnames are the same as our family names may descend from the slaves of our ancestors. We know that slaves were often abused and exploited by their owners. Several slave descendants have contacted me regarding our shared DNA. I welcome and embrace them, just as I welcome all of the DNA cousins who contact me and look forward to trying to discover our shared ancestors.

Speaking of DNA, I have found it to be a useful tool to test the validity of my historical research. People who have their DNA tested often find their ancestry composition contains links to populations they hadn't expected. I wanted to learn what our family's DNA told about us, so in 2010, I ordered test kits though the DNA testing company 23andMe for myself, my brother (Bud Watson), representing our paternal ancestors, and our maternal uncle (Bud Walker). Although I wouldn't have minded finding some surprises in our DNA, what I learned is that our genomes closely match what I have learned about our genealogy.

We know from our family history that most of our ancestors came to the American colonies from England, Ireland and Scotland. A few came from France, Germany and Switzerland. We know that many of our English ancestors came from Normandy (France) after the Norman Conquest in 1066. Normandy was settled by Vikings from Scandinavia.

A summary of our DNA results confirm what history has outlined: we are between 50 and 60 percent English, Scottish and Irish, and between 18 and 24 percent French, German and Scandinavian.

Rounding out the composition is a vague designation of between 14 and 21 percent broadly Northwestern European and a little Scandinavian and Italian.

I have not found ancestors with Italian surnames, but there are several reasons why we might have some Italian DNA. These include the proximity of our German-speaking

ANCESTRY COMPOSITION 23andMe	
Roberta Watson Richardson	**100%**
European	99.9%
British & Irish	59.8%
United Kingdom	
French & German	18.0%
Switzerland	
Scandinavian	5.9%
Italian	0.5%
Broadly Northwestern European	14.1%
Broadly Southern European	0.7%
Broadly European	0.9%

Swiss ancestors to the Italian-speaking areas or a possible confirmation of our link to the sons of Tancred de Hauteville who ruled southern Italy from the 11th to 13th centuries (see the profile for Anthony Toncray). As DNA research advances, it will be interesting to see what we may learn in the future.

While our DNA doesn't confirm it, there are a few Natives in both Walker and Watson family trees. In every case, the connection comes about because of relationships with Europeans, which means that Native DNA is greatly diluted by the time it gets to our generation.

You might question my choice to include a chapter about our Native ancestors in a book about immigrants, but if you know their history, you know that they were forced to leave their homelands and settle elsewhere to make room for European settlers. They were immigrants and refugees against their will. Their stories tell of strength, courage, wisdom and leadership in the face of insurmountable adversity.

I am grateful to all of the DNA cousins who have contacted me over the past few years. As yet, DNA testing hasn't revealed much more than general information about our nationalities. It does show, however, that I have 4 percent Neanderthal ancestry, more than 69 percent of 23andMe customers. I'm not sure what that implies, but I'm as proud of my Neanderthal ancestors as I am of all the others. I am hopeful that as the research continues, DNA information will become more useful in pinpointing specific genealogic, historic and geographic details.

Even more so, I am grateful to all of the genealogists, historians and researchers who generously share their findings online so we all may trace our family histories. When I first started my research nearly 25 years ago, most records had to be ordered from various government and historical research facilities. Now infinite numbers of resources are available online to make research accessible to anyone interested in tracing their family history.

A tribute and travel guide

I want to make it clear that this book is not a genealogy book—it is a tribute to my immigrant ancestors. It is a resource and a guide for people who want to learn about their immigrant ancestors and explore their roots in other countries. To that end, I've added notes and visitor information about many of the castles and estates connected to our family heritage. I want to encourage others who would like to know about the origins of their immigrant ancestors to explore their roots and enrich their visit by learning about the places their ancestors lived or are connected to their family history.

Because this is not a genealogy book, I've left out many of the dates and qualifying data that genealogists rely on. If researchers want to argue about some of the information in this book, talk among yourselves. Think about my book as the "CliffsNotes" of our family history. The information I've recorded is supported by years of genealogical research and I have more than 15,000 people in my Walker and Watson family trees on ancestry.com along with the data to back up the research. I eliminated footnotes within the text because I feel they are distracting, but I've included an extensive bibliography at the end of the book for anyone interested in checking my sources.

Most of this book was researched using online resources. A single Google search often will reveal dozens of options for research. Wikipedia is a valuable research tool that condenses random facts about a subject into one easily accessible article. I usually don't stop there though. I look at the Wikipedia references and check such resources as Google Books, which offers access to millions of free books on every imaginable subject.

Family history research can be intimidating to the newcomer, but for those who are willing to take the time and effort to dig for the details, it is an enriching and rewarding enterprise. There are numerous family history websites online. I've found that ancestry.com offers the most comprehensive collection of resources and guides but there are many free sites that can provide similar services. I encourage you to give it a try and to learn about how your family connects to places where you may travel. Knowing that members of your family may have walked the same paths that you are following makes the journey all the more fulfilling.

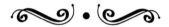

Provenance *is dedicated to immigrants everywhere who courageously leave their homelands to build better lives for themselves and their families. Their courage, foresight and hard work are the building blocks on which societies was founded.*

Origins

Whenever I hear people complain about how immigration is ruining America, I have to wonder—where do they think they came from? Unless they are Natives, they are descended from immigrants. America was founded by immigrants who worked together to build a strong and bountiful nation.

Our family probably has more immigrant ancestors than most—I've identified about 90 in this book and there are others I haven't been able to trace. Our family lines go way back to some of America's first settlers in Jamestown, Virginia, or even further when you count our Native ancestors. I've included a few notable Natives in this book because they were unwilling immigrants, forced to leave their homelands to make way for European settlers.

Our online family history records on ancestry.com are organized into two trees to better manage thousands of records. My father's Watson Family Tree [https://www.ancestry.com/family-tree/tree/33134704/family] represents paternal ancestors. Note that the Watson list is much longer than the Walker line because more of them arrived in the earliest days of the colonies. My mother's Walker Family Tree [https://www.ancestry.com/family-tree/tree/15313302/family] are maternal ancestors. In this list and throughout the book, I will maintain those distinctions. However, the lines are not always that clear cut because our Watson and Walker lines crossed in the early 1700s, so some names appear on both family trees.

Relationships of individuals listed throughout the book are to my generation. If you are related to me, you can determine your relationship by adding a year for each subsequent generation. That is, my 10th great-grandmother is my son's 11th great-grandmother, and my grandson's 12th great-grandmother.

Watson Immigrant Ancestors

From England to Virginia	*Arrival*
Agnes Barrett (1630-1690) 8th great-grandmother	1648
Sir Francis Barrett (1600-1656) 9th great-grandfather	1623
Mary Bostick (1670-1717) 6th great-grandmother	1684
William Bostick (1654-1739) 7th great-grandfather	1684
Thomas Pasmere Carpenter (1607-1675) 9th great-grandfather	1627
Robert Coleman (1622-1682) 7th great-grandfather	1637

From England to Virginia (continued)   Arrival
Henry Corbin (1629-1675) 11th great-grandfather   1654
Katherine Croshaw (1586-1636) 8th great-grandmother   1610
Capt. Raleigh Croshaw (1560-1624) 10th great-grandfather   1608
John Davis (1599-1678) 9th great-grandfather   1623
Mary Denham (1598-1646) 9th great-grandmother   1623
Alice Eltonhead (1627-1684) 11th great-grandmother   1654
John English (1599-1678) 9th great-grandfather   1624
Capt Thomas Graves (1584-1635) 8th great-grandfather   1607
Elizabeth Gorusch (1618-1704) 8th great-grandmother   1630
William Grizzell (1600-1636) 8th great-grandfather   bef 1630
William P. Grizzle (1570-1636) 9th great-grandfather   bef 1630
Mary Anne Jolliffe (1620-1670) 8th great-grandmother   1637
William Leake (1664-1725) 6th great-grandfather   bef 1684
Elizabeth Mainwaring (1580-1647) 9th great-grandmother   1637
Thomas Mask (1600-1687) 8th great-grandfather   bef 1672
Governor Samuel Matthews (1583-1660) 9th great-grandfather   1619
Richard New (1620-1680) 8th great-grandfather   1637
Francis Place (1610-1655) 8th great-grandfather   bef 1637
Thomas Powell (1599-1687) 10th great-grandfather   1609
William Powell (1569-1623) 9th great-grandfather   1609
Lucretia Ripley (1604-1636) 8th great-grandmother   bef 1624
John Talley (1593-1660) 13th great-grandfather   bef 1645
Nathan Talley (1624-1710) 12th great-grandfather   bef 1645
John "Rocky Creek" Watson (1740-1810) 4th great-grandfather   1754
Joseph Watson (1705-?) 5th great-grandfather   1754
John Watts (1638-1703) 9th great-grandfather   1660
Ann Williamson (1617-1655) 8th great-grandmother   bef 1637
Elizabeth Wyllys (1598-1635) 10th great-grandmother   1618

From England to Massachusetts   Arrival
Elizabeth Wooley (1603-1676) 8th great-grandmother   bef 1650

From Scotland to Virginia   Arrival
William John Mackgahee (1618-1675) 10th great-grandfather   1653

From Scotland to Virginia and North Carolina   Arrival
William Black (1693-1782) 6th great-grandfather   1735
Eleanor Helen Mathie Metland (1682-1740) 6th great grandmother   1735

From Scotland to Virginia and South Carolina   Arrival
Robert Black (1718-1799) 4th great-grandfather   1735

From Scotland to Massachusetts   Arrival
John Maguffey (1605-1665) 8th great-grandfather   bef 1650

	Arrival
From Isle of Man to Virginia	
Thomas Christian I (1636-1694) 7th great-grandfather	1657
Elinor Kewley (1640-1688) 7th great-grandmother	bef 1663
From Isle of Man or England to Louisiana	*Arrival*
William Peter Christian (1816-1878) great-grandfather	bef 1840
From Ireland to South Carolina	*Arrival*
James Bell (1774-1870) 3rd great-grandfather	bef 1800
Joseph Elias Carroll (1699-1784) 5th great-grandfather	1735
Elizabeth Margaret McClellan (1737-1778) 5th great-grandmother	bef 1752
Jennet Jane Swansey (1710-1784) 5th great-grandmother	1735
James Swancey (1737-1780) 5th great-grandfather	bef 1752
From Ireland to Virginia	*Arrival*
John C. Coffey (1620-1713) 7th great-grandfather	1637
Capt. Richard Pearis (1725-1794) 5th great-grandfather	1740
From Ireland to Pennsylvania Quaker colony	*Arrival*
Elizabeth Duck (1660-1712) 8th great-grandmother	1687
Ezekiel Harlan Sr (1679-1731) 6th great-grandfather	1687
George Harlan (1649-1714) 7th great-grandfather	1687
William Oborn (1645-1684) 7th great-grandfather	1679
From England to Pennsylvania Quaker colony	*Arrival*
Richard Buffington (1655-1748) 7th great-grandfather	bef 1676
Ruth Buffington (1682-1744) 6th great-grandmother	bef 1676
Ann Francis (1652-1697) 7th great-grandmother	bef 1676
Hannah Cooke (1682-1766) 6th great-grandmother	abt 1688
William Cooke (1637-1688) 8th great-grandfather	bef 1663
Mary Skeate (1634-?) 7th great-grandmother	1679
From Germany to Tennessee	*Arrival*
Zene Turner (1810-?) 3rd great-grandfather	bef 1830
From Eastern to Western Cherokee Nation	*Arrival*
William Crawford Beatty (1825-) 2nd great-grandfather	1838
Mary "Polly" Langley (1802-1851) 3rd great-grandmother	1832
Emaline Parris (1827-1906) 2nd great-grandmother	1832
Moses "Tu-Lu-Squit" Parris (1788-1865) 3rd great-grandfather	1832
Joseph Phillips Sr. (1786-1876) 4th great-grandfather	1838
Sarah "Sallie" Phillips (1808-1866) 3rd great-grandmother	1838

Walker Immigrant Ancestors

From England to Virginia	*Arrival*
Katherine Royall Banks (1610-1686) 10th great-grandmother	bef 1642
Agnes Barrett (1628-1690) 8th great-grandmother	abt 1648
Francis Barrett (1600-1656) 9th great-grandfather	1623
Margaret [Unknown] Barrett (1600-1680) 9th great-grandmother	1630
Mary Brett (1603-1682) 11th great-grandmother	aft 1631
Giles Carter (1634-1701) 8th great-grandfather	1653
James Crewes (1610-1677) 9th great-grandfather	abt 1650
Jane Hanks (1603-?) 9th great-grandmother	bef 1629
Capt Henry Isham (1627-1678) 10th great-grandfather	1656
Henry Isham (1650-1675) 9th great-grandfather	1656
Richard New (1620-1680) 8th great-grandfather	1637
Colonel William Randolph (1651-1711) 8th great-grandfather	1672
John Richard Webb (1603-1662) 9th great-grandfather	1626
John Webb (1659-1726) 7th great-grandfather	1626
William Webb (1588-1656) 10th great-grandfather	1626

From England to Massachusetts	*Arrival*
Alexander Webb Jr (1559-1629) 11th great-grandfather	1626

From Germany to Pennsylvania	*Arrival*
Johan Jurg Meisser (1680-1745) 7th great-grandfather	1709
Johann Michael Meiser (1703-1705) 6th great-grandfather	1709
Anna Elizabeth Sixt (1694-1745) 6th great-grandmother	bef 1723

From France or host country to New York	*Arrival*
Anthony W. Toncray (Tancre) (1710-1779) 6th great-grandfather	1736

From France or host country to Virginia	*Arrival*
Pierre Tule (1660-?) 7th great-grandfather	1701

From Switzerland to California	*Arrival*
Frank X. Walker (1860-1935) great-grandfather	1881

From Ireland to California	*Arrival*
Thomas Wallace (1836-1886) 2nd great-grandfather	abt 1840

VIRGINIANS

Most Americans think that Thanksgiving is a day to celebrate the feast shared by Natives and Pilgrims, who were the first settlers in America. But they weren't the first. Some of our family's immigrant ancestors were living in Virginia more than a decade before the Pilgrims even left England. Our first families of American immigrants—the Barretts, Croshaws, Davises, Graves, Matthews and Powells—all arrived in Virginia before 1620.

The history of England's attempts to establish settlements in Virginia began in 1585 when Queen Elizabeth I chartered Sir Walter Raleigh's ill-fated Roanoke colony. Spanish ships blocked supplies for the venture, so the settlers were gone by the time someone finally arrived to rescue them. Theories abound but no one really knows what happened to the Roanoke settlers.

King James I, who succeeded Elizabeth, signed a peace treaty with Spain in 1604 that promised to end attacks on ships from both countries. For wealthy English venture capitalists, that meant it was safe to cross the Atlantic again. Land and resources were free for the picking, and James was happy to encourage private developers who promised to enrich his coffers with taxes on the gold and silver they expected to find there. The catch was that they had to finance their ventures themselves.

The investors established The Virginia Company of London as a joint-stock venture that sold shares to finance a colony on the James River called Jamestown. We know that some of our ancestors were among those original "Adventurers" or stockholders. In 1607, 104 members of the company, their sons and workers, arrived in three ships to start the Jamestown settlement.

Those first settlers were used to comfortable lives in England. They went to Virginia thinking that all they had to do was scoop up the gold and silver and bring it home. They soon learned there was no gold, and pampered rich men didn't have a chance of surviving in the wilderness. Many of the first settlers died before more ships and settlers could arrive.

Meanwhile, the investors in England were enticing more settlers with the riches awaiting them in Virginia. Even while the first ones were dying, new ones already were on the way. Some of them must have been more stalwart than the first group because they managed to survive with the help of sympathetic Powhatan Natives.

The new arrivals brought tobacco seeds, which proved to be a successful cash crop to trade with England and the Natives for goods and services. In 1619, the Virginia Company recruited and shipped over 90 women to become wives and start families in Virginia.

In the early years, the Powhatans had been friendly and generous with the settlers, but the English soon began demanding more than they could or wanted to provide. As plantations and settlements continued to intrude on Powhatan hunting grounds, the Natives said "Enough!" and began attacking the English.

The attacks by Natives plus dwindling funds and internal feuding finally tipped the London Company into bankruptcy. In 1625, King James revoked the charter and Virginia became a royal colony, which it remained until the Revolutionary War.

Despite Native uprisings that killed about 350 colonists and destroyed several plantations, tobacco harvests continued to increase yearly. The colony shipped about 40,000 pounds in 1618. By the 1730s, production topped 34 million pounds.

As production increased, the demand for workers increased as well. In the 1600s, some of our immigrant ancestors arrived as indentured servants. They worked for a fixed number of years to pay for their passage and then became free. Under the headright system, planters and merchants promised land to entice workers.

Captain John Smith created the first detailed map of the Chesapeake Region. His map of Virginia, published in 1612 opened this part of North America to European exploration, settlement, and trade.

By the beginning of the 1700s, the number of indentured servants dwindled and the need for workers was largely met by enslaved Africans, a practice that continued until President Abraham Lincoln signed the Emancipation Proclamation in 1863. Even then, slaves in Texas, where many of our Virginia ancestors had resettled during the 1700s, didn't learn about their freedom until 1865.

As Virginia's tobacco industry increased, so did its population. The colony grew rapidly from about 400 settlers in 1620 to 10,400 in 1640. By 1780, it had the largest population in the colonies with nearly 540,000 residents, including more than 220,000 slaves.

Most of our Watson and Walker ancestors arrived in Virginia before 1700. They came from every walk of life—as "second sons" of wealthy landowners, as adventurers, as indentured servants and a few to escape religious persecution.

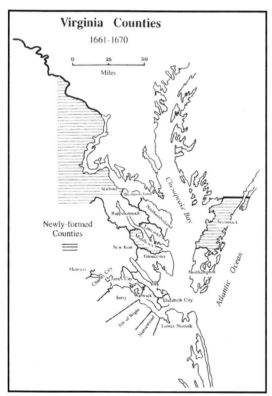

Virginia grew rapidly from about 400 settlers in 1620 to 10,400 in 1640. By 1780, it had the largest population in the colonies with nearly 540,000 residents.

It was a law in England that only the eldest sons of landowners and the nobility could inherit property, so younger sons had to find other ways to earn a living. Many were sent to Virginia to enhance their families' holdings. If this history seems to be focused on individuals from wealthy or prominent families, that's because they have the most thoroughly documented family histories. The histories of those who arrived from poorer families are far harder to research. For every story I have documented, there are as many or more that remain untold because their histories were not recorded or records were lost over the centuries.

Earliest Arrivals

These immigrant ancestors helped to build the Jamestown settlement. They had already claimed land in Virginia and were developing their plantations before the Pilgrims arrived at Plymouth Rock in 1620.

Francis and Agnes Barrett
Francis is 10th great-grandfather Watson line, 9th Walker line; Agnes 9th Watson great-grandmother, 8th Walker line

The remarkable thing about the Barretts is that they are proof that our Watson and Walker families were linked from the earliest days of American history. Agnes Barrett is believed to be the wife of Richard New, whose daughters Rebecca and Elizabeth married, respectively, our ancestors Thomas Christian II on the Watson side, and John Tuley (Tully) on the Walker side.

Francis Barrett was among 120 people who sailed for the Virginia Colony in 1619 aboard the English ship Bona Nova. The ship was commanded by Capt. John Huddleston and the voyage was sponsored by the Virginia Company.

A ship's roll for the Bona Nova includes "Barrett, Francis—muster at Hog Island as servant to Lt. Barkley." I have not found a Lt. Barkley among lists of early Virginia residents. It is very likely that Francis Barrett was sent to manage the Berkeley family's property in Virginia.

Castle Barrett in Cork, Ireland, now in ruins, was acquired by the Barrett family in the 17th century.

The Berkeleys of Scotland are believed to have descended from the Earls of Berkeley, who built Berkeley Castle in Gloucestershire, England, in 1153. The Berkeleys were prominent among Virginia's first families. Sir William Berkeley was appointed governor of Virginia by King Charles II of England and served from 1660 to 1667.

Agnes Barrett is believed to be the daughter of Francis Barrett, although records indicate that she was born in Bristol, Gloucestershire, England, and Francis Barrett was in Virginia by 1620. However, if Francis Barrett was managing property for the Berkeleys, it is possible that he returned to England from time to time.

Francis Barrett is thought to have married Margaret (unknown) in Charles City County, Virginia, in 1630. Agnes may have been a child from a previous marriage or she may have been Margaret's child.

It is generally believed that the Barretts are descendants of the Normans who took over English estates after the Battle of Hastings in 1066. Halsted's *History of Kent* states that the ancestor of the Barrett family is recorded in the Battle Abbey Roll as one of those who came over with William the Conqueror.

The earliest example of a Barrett landowner is Gamel Baret of Yorkshire in the *Domesday Book*, a 1086 survey of English landowners. From the 12th century, Barretts were recorded in Suffolk, Bedford, Cambridge and Norfolk counties in England, and in the counties of Limerick, Cork and Dublin in Ireland.

Castle Barrett, now in ruins, was built around the 13th century in Mallow, County Cork, Ireland. Originally known as Castle More or Castlemore, the Barrett family acquired the castle in the 17th century. The castle was damaged in 1645 by Oliver Cromwell's army. After the Battle of the Boyne in 1690, John Barrett, who fought on the side of the Jacobites, lost to the Williamites. Castle Barrett was destroyed and 12,000 acres of Barrett land were forfeited.

Belhus mansion is another famous landmark connected to the Barrett family. In 1405, John Barrett of Hawkherst, Kent, married Alice Belhouse who inherited Belhouse (now Belhus), the seat of her father, Thomas Belhouse, as well as extensive manors in Essex in the Parish of Avely. Belhus now is a golf course, country park and part of the Thames Chase woodland.

Belhus now is a golfcourse, country park and part of the Thames Chase woodland.

Famous Barretts include English poet Elizabeth Barrett Browning and Irish and English landscape painters George Barret Sr. and George Barret Jr.

Capt. Raleigh Croshaw and Katherine Croshaw
10th great-grandfather and 9th great-grandmother, Watson line

When the family history is as confusing and unlikely as what many researchers have attributed to Capt. Raleigh Croshaw, I generally just say to myself, "We have enough ancestors. This doesn't make any sense—we can do without him."

However, Raleigh Croshaw is too interesting to just delete from the family tree because I can't be sure about his origins. He was one of the very first people to arrive at Jamestown, Virginia. He arrived on "Mary & Margaret," the second supply ship, in September 1608. I'm fairly sure we are related through Katherine Croshaw, the wife of Capt. Thomas Graves. I'm not sure whether she is his daughter, which makes him my 10th great-grandfather, or his sister, which would make him a great-uncle.

Whatever the details of his relationship to our family, Raleigh Croshaw is important to the history of the Jamestown settlement in Virginia. He is designated as an "Ancient planter" for being among the first colonists to receive land grants in Virginia and served as a representative in the House of Burgesses for Elizabeth City County in the Virginia colony and Dominion of Virginia.

Capt. Croshaw was known to have been skilled at fighting the Natives. He was mentioned as being a member of the group with Capt. John Smith in January 1609 who were attempting to trade for corn at the village of Powhatan Chief Opechancanough. The settlers would have been overcome by a surprise attack by members of the tribe were it not for quick reactions on the part of Raleigh Croshaw.

At the time of the 1622 massacre, Raleigh Croshaw was on a trading mission and successfully defended a remote trading outpost. Jamestown was warned and saved from the surprise attack but about 400 English settlers living in small communities—a third of the population of Virginia Colony—were killed by Natives during the attack.

What now is known as Williamsburg, Virginia, originally was Elizabeth City and later Middle Plantation. Raleigh Croshaw was the local official in the Elizabeth City area. His sons (or brothers) Joseph and Richard were among the first to take advantage of this new settlement and are mentioned many times in the records. Joseph appears to have led a more public life, having been a member of the House of Burgesses from York as well as having served as a justice and as sheriff for York County, Virginia.

Researchers seem to have reached something of a consensus regarding this rough outline of Raleigh Croshaw's life in Virginia. There are some other important details that are harder to sort out, though. What bothers me the most is how many researchers are willing to believe that he was born in 1540. That would have made him nearly 70 years old when he arrived in Virginia and began trading and fighting with the Natives. Life expectancy was only about 35 years in the 1500s and under 25 years in Jamestown. Even accepting 1570 as his birth date stretched my credulity, but I want this guy in our family tree, so I'm giving him some leeway.

What is harder to sort out is who were his wives and children. There are records that show his wife arrived in Virginia in 1620 aboard the "Bona Nova" and died in Virginia in 1624. I believe that this woman may have been a first wife and mother of Katherine, Richard and Joseph, who were born in England and came to Jamestown with him. Some say she was Unity Ursula Daniels, others say her name was Katherine, and some say Rachel.

What now is known as Williamsburg, Virginia, originally was Elizabeth City and later Middle Plantation. Raleigh Croshaw was the local official in the Elizabeth City area.

Others claim that Raleigh Croshaw's wife, or second wife, was a Native woman, the daughter of the chief of the Patawomeck tribe, possibly a sister to Powahatan. A claimed descendant believes her name was Ursula Unity Patawomeck and that they had at least five children: Richard, Joseph, Benjamin, Noah and Ursala Unity. So you see the difficulty.

It seems likely that the family may have come from the little village of Crawshawbooth, Lancashire, England. Any recorded history about the place apparently occurred after the Croshaws left for the colonies—the oldest building there is a Quaker Meeting House built in the 1700s.

Our Crowshaw ancestors' migration to America must have nearly cleared Crawshawbooth of Croshaws. There are only about 800 people named Crowshaw or a variant of it in the world today, most in the United States. The name probably comes from the Old English "crawa," meaning crow, and "sceaga," a grove or thicket. In the Middle Ages, when tax collectors created the need for surnames, people often adopted the name of their village, so names like "de Percy, meaning "of Percy" developed. The first recorded spelling of the Crowshaw name is John de Crouschagh, dated 1308 in the Wakefield Manor Court Rolls in York during the reign of King Edward II.

John Davis
9th great-grandfather, Watson line

John Davis was 24 years old when he arrived in Virginia in 1623 aboard the ship "John and Francis." A Capt. Thomas Davis also arrived on the same ship in 1623. Some researchers believe that John was Thomas' son. However, other research suggests that his parents were John Thomas Rhys Davis and Elizabeth Betsy Lawrence of Gloustershire. It is likely that Thomas Davis was a relative but not his father.

We don't know why John Davis went to the colonies, but he probably was seeking greater opportunities than were available in 17th century England, which was embroiled in religious and economic turmoil. He was not listed as a servant on the ship muster, so he may have assisted Capt. Davis to pay for his passage or found some other way to pay for the crossing.

John was among residents of Isle of Wight County who participated in, then recanted their support for Bacon's Rebellion, an armed rebellion against Governor Berkeley. Their statement said, "We, the subscribed, having drawn up a paper in behalf of the inhabitants of Isle of Wight county as to the grievances of the said county recant all the false and scandalous reflection upon Governor, Sir William Berkeley, contained in a paper presented to the commissioners and promise never to be guilty again of the like mutinous and rebellious practices."

Although it's clear that John Davis was in Isle of Wight County, I have not found evidence that he was a landowner. Several land grants were made to Thomas Davis however, so it is possible that John was employed by Capt. Davis.

John married Mary Polly Denham (or Durham), who is believed to also have come to Virginia from Gloucestershire. Records indicate that they were married in Virginia in about 1625 and had at least seven children.

Many Davis researchers have connected our Davis line to Dafydd ap Gruffyd, who was Prince of Wales in 1282-1283. Somehow, those researchers seem to have overlooked the fact that about three generations are missing in their family trees between John Dafydd ap Gualiter Davis, who was born in 1347, and Dafydd ap Gruffydd, who died in 1283. While it may be possible that we are related to this royal line, which also includes the Tudor kings, until those three generations are identified, we won't know. Other prominent Davises include Jefferson Davis, the President of the Confederate States of America during the Civil War.

John English
10th great-grandfather, Watson line

Seal of the Jamestowne Society

Who was John English? I know he was my 10th great-grandfather, but after considerable research, I don't know much else. About his only distinction is being named a qualifying member of the Jamestown Society, an organization dedicated to honoring the descendants of "early settlers who lived or held colonial government positions in Jamestowne, Virginia, prior to 1700, or who invested in its establishment."

Early records show that John English arrived in Jamestown in about 1624 and lived on the Isle of Wight, where there also lived a William English, who also is listed as a qualifying member and two other men with the surname English, Richard and Francis, who are not on the list. John was a member of the Virginia House of Burgess in 1659 and his will was proved in Isle of Wight County in 1678.

John English could have married his wife, Frances, in England or in Virginia—researchers disagree on this. I believe they married in Virginia, because men so outnumbered women in the colonies, many women went there with the explicit purpose of finding a husband. Records show they had at least seven children between 1634 and 1645.

Most researchers believe that he was born in Horsham, Sussex, England, in about 1599. Horsham was known for horse trading in early medieval times, then iron and brick making until the 20th century, and brewing more recently. His father was Richard English and his grandfather has been identified as "Sir" Richard English of Warwickshire, However, I'm fairly certain he was not the Earl of Warwick and I can't find evidence of other reasons he might have had such a title.

John English's daughter, Alice English, was born in Virginia and married John Watts, an English immigrant who probably arrived as an indentured servant and lived in Isle of Wight, Virginia. There were about 30 Watts who arrived in Virginia between 1636 and 1656.

There is little recorded history about Alice's husband John and other early Watts families in Virginia, but some who could have been their descendants led interesting lives among the Cherokee. A John Watts was a mixed-blood son of a British trader, also named John Watts, who was one of the leaders of the Chickamauga Cherokee during the Cherokee-American wars from 1788 to 1794. Chief John Watts, his wife, children and much of his extended family were killed in a British-inspired attack by Cherokee mercenaries in 1798.

Capt. Thomas Graves
9th great-grandfather, Watson line

Thomas Graves was one of the original Adventurers or stockholders of the Virginia Company of London, and one of the founders of Jamestown. He arrived in October 1608 on the colony's second supply ship, "Mary and Margaret."

Capt. Graves apparently returned to England, where he married Katherine Croshaw and fathered several of their children before he returned to Virginia. He was not

The official seal of the Virginia Company of London shows King James, and has the word Virginia (in Latin spelling) around a crest.

Thomas Graves was one of the original Adventurers or stockholders of the Virginia Company of London, and one of the founders of Jamestown.

in Jamestown during "the starving time," the winter of 1609-1610, when food shortages, fractured leadership and attacks by Natives killed all but 60 of 300 colonists.

On his return, Capt. Graves settled at Smythe's Hundred, a plantation on the James River ten miles from Jamestown. He is among a distinguished list of 150 original land-owners in Virginia called "Ancient Planters." Smythe's Hundred was abandoned after a Native uprising in 1622. In 1627, he was commissioned to command the Plantation at Accomac. He patented property there and lived on Old Plantation Creek, now in Northampton County, Virginia. Capt. Graves and Katherine Croshaw had six children: John, Thomas, Ann, Verlinda, Katherine and Francis. Our line descends through Francis. Capt. Graves' daughter, Verlinda, married William Stone, the governor of Maryland.

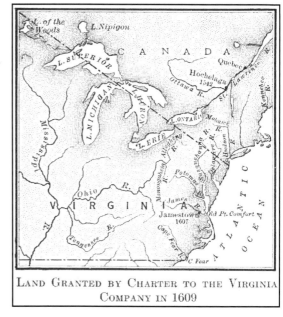

LAND GRANTED BY CHARTER TO THE VIRGINIA COMPANY IN 1609

Thomas Graves was a member of the First Legislative Assembly in America and appears on a monument to the first House of Burgesses which stands in Jamestown today. He was designated as "Esquire," which indicates that he may have been a member of the Governor's Council. He was recorded as being a justice at the court held in Accomac in 1635.

The original Hungar Church built by Capt. Graves was replaced in 1742 by a brick structure that is still standing and in use today.

On orders from Jamestown in 1635, Capt. Graves and the Rev. William Cotton were ordered to form a vestry and build a church on "the north side of Hungars Creek." The original 40-foot-long wooden church built in 1679 was replaced in 1742 by a brick structure that is still standing and holding services to this day. Now known as Hungars Episcopal Church, it is located at Bridgetown, Northampton County, Virginia.

Capt. Graves also was directed by the assembly to establish a burying ground on the church grounds. The cemetery is still there along with a large memorial monument to Thomas Graves, who died in 1636.

Ancestors of Thomas Graves probably were Normans who went to England after the Conquest in 1066. Members have been recorded as de Grevis, de Greves, Greve, Grave, Greaves, Greeves and Graves. A variation of the name, Greue, was recorded in *The Domesday Book* of 1086 in Lincolnshire, and other variations later in the counties of Nottingham, Derby and York.

According to *Burke's Landed Gentry* of 1838, "The first [Greaves] . . . of whom we possess any authentic record is Les Greaves who was settled at Beeley and Greaves as early as the reign of King Henry I (years 1100-1135), from which time until the end of the 17th century, his descendants continued to reside there."

The Greaves manor house in Beeley, Derbyshire, was renamed Beeley Hilltop in the 17th century.

Today, Beeley, Derbyshire, is a picturesque village with a few reminders of the Greaves family. The building now known as Beeley Old Hall, opposite the Norman House in the village, is believed to have been the Greaves manor house until they moved to a house, called "The Greaves." Following Greaves' death in 1621, the Old Hall and the manor house were both rebuilt and the latter, where the arms of King James I can still be seen above a bedroom mantelpiece, was renamed Beeley Hilltop. Both reverted to farmhouse status late in the 17th century, and in 1747 Beeley Hill Top was purchased by the 3rd Duke of Devonshire.

Samuel Matthew
10th great-grandfather, Watson line

Samuel Matthew arrived in Virginia in 1619. He established a plantation, "Mathews Manor," later known as Denbigh, which was located on the north side of the James River at Blunt Point, the confluence of the Warwick and James rivers in the area which later became Warwick County, Virginia.

Samuel was the third son of the eminent English prelate, Tobias Matthew. Tobias, the son of a Bristol merchant, became a student at University of Oxford beginning in 1558 at the age of 13. Attracting the favorable notice of Queen Elizabeth I, his career rose steadily from president of St. John's College, Oxford, in 1572 through a succession of academic appointments to become Archbishop of York in 1606.

Tobias Matthew's wife, and Samuel's mother, was Frances Barlow, who could claim that her father was a bishop, her father-in-law archbishop, her four brothers all bishops and her husband an archbishop. Tobias and Frances had three sons, Tobias, John and Samuel. Archbishop Matthew, who was known as a great wit, is said to have told Lord Fairfax, when asked why he was so pensive, "My lord, I have great reason for sorrow with respect to my sons. One of them has wit and no grace, the other grace but no wit, and the third neither grace nor wit."

The eldest son, Tobias II, was highly educated but a disappointment to his parents because he converted to Catholicism while visiting in Italy. He found favor with the English court, however, and was honored with knighthood by James I in 1623. When the religious wars broke out in England, Tobias II was suspected of being a spy for the Church of Rome. He left the country and joined the Jesuits in Flanders, where he died in 1655. Tobias' second son, John, seems to have slipped into the oblivion of history, but our ancestor, his third son, Samuel, may have won his parents' favor through his success as a planter in Colonial Virginia.

Samuel Mathew built Mathews Manor, later renamed Denbigh Plantation, around 1626. This photo of the Denbigh Plantation springhouse was taken in the 1930s.

Known as Col. Matthew, he added several other land holdings and became one of the most prominent men in the Jamestown colony. By 1621 he was a member of the Governor's Council and played an active role in resolving conflicts with Natives in the area. In 1635, he was a leader in the mutiny that ousted Royal Governor John Harvey, appointed by King Charles I. Samuel Matthew and three others were charged with treason and sent home to England to stand trial. The charges eventually were dropped and Matthew returned to Virginia in 1639 and resumed service on the Governor's Council until 1644.

Samuel married the twice-widowed Frances Grevill, who brought with her to the marriage considerable wealth from the estates of her first two husbands. They had two sons, Samuel and Francis. Our family descends from a third child, Mary Ann Matthew, who probably was the product of an earlier marriage for Samuel as her birth date is before he immigrated to Virginia and married Frances Grevill. Mary Ann remained in England, where she married Thomas Buffington, father of our ancestor, the immigrant Richard Buffington (see Refugees: Quaker).

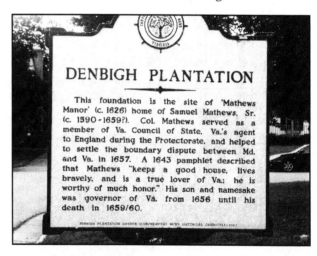

The younger Samuel was known as Lt. Col. Samuel Matthews as an adult (at some point, an "s" was added to the surname), reflecting his role in the local militia. He was named a representative to the Virginia House of Burgesses in 1652, to the Governor's Council in 1656, and later that year, became the Commonwealth Governor of Virginia, a position held until his death in January 1660. Samuel II's brother, Francis, was a tobacco planter who had a large estate of some 2000 acres in Northumberland County, Virginia.

Col. Mathew built Mathews Manor around 1626. The site of Mathews Manor, located within the independent city of Newport News, Virginia, was the subject of an archaeological study led by Colonial Williamsburg's Ivor Noel Hume in the 1960s, and was placed on the National Park Service's National Register of Historic Places.

William and Thomas Powell
12th and 10th great-grandfathers, Watson line

Capt. William Powell and his grandson, Thomas, arrived in Jamestown in the third supply mission of nine ships that brought additional settlers and supplies to the surviving colonists in 1609. He soon distinguished himself by killing the chief of a tribe of Natives that were threatening the colonists. Powell was appointed a captain and became responsible for the Jamestown defenses. In 1617, he was appointed lieutenant governor of the colony.

In 1622, William Powell secured rights to establish a large plantation on the Chickahominy River, which places him among a small group of Virginians referred to as an "Ancient Planter." John Powell, Thomas Powell's brother, also is on the list, but for some reason, Thomas is not. The list applies to colonists who migrated to the Virginia colony when it was managed by the Virginia Company of London. William Powell was a subscriber to the company. The "Ancient Planters" received land grants if they stayed in the colony for at least three years. Under the terms of the "Instructions to Governor Yeardley" (issued by the London Company in 1618), these colonists received the first land grants in Virginia.

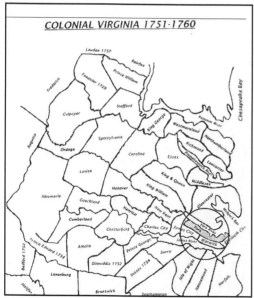

Virginia counties about 1750. The Powells were said to have owned the whole of York County at one time.

Shortly after beginning the plantation project, he was killed leading a party of militia against the Natives. His widow, Margaret Powell, married Edward Blaney, a James City County burgess, in 1623.

The above information is well documented. Other than these details, there isn't much consensus among Powell researchers. There were many Powells in early Virginia and most of them were named William, John or Thomas.

As near as I can determine, we descend from Capt. William Powell and his grandson, Thomas Powell. We are indirectly related to William's brother, the immigrant Capt. Nathanial Powell and John Powell, who could be either Thomas' father or brother. Records show that John Powell was born and died in England.

Could Thomas' father be the Capt. John Powell who was the first governor of the Isle of Barbados under English rule? It is certainly possible that he could have claimed Barbados for the King then sailed on to Virginia and returned to England before his death.

How or if all of the Powells in Virginia were related is unclear, but they all seem to have been from successful English families. The following is an excerpt from *Historical Sketches of the Campbell, Pilcher and Kindred Families* by Margaret Campbell Pilcher, published in 1911:

> *The first mention of the name in connection with America was Sgt. Major Anthony Powell, who was killed at St. Augustine in 1586, in the expedition of Sir Frances Drake against the Spaniards.*
>
> *One Captain John Powell was the first Governor of the Isle of Barbados under English rule. The Powells were among the earliest and wealthiest ship owners and commanders in the colonies. One Anthony Powell was military commander of Sir Walter Raleigh's colonists who landed in America in 1583 at Roanoke Island, where Raleigh was built. Powell's Point on the coast was named in his honor.*
>
> *Captain Nathaniel Powell, who came to Jamestown, Virginia colony, in 1607, wrote much of John Smith's History of Virginia, and it was he who made the first map of Virginia, sending it back to England, where it is now preserved in the British Museum.*
>
> *The land upon which Williamsburg, Virginia, was built was first deeded to Benjamin Powell by the King of England. Captains William and Nathaniel Powell had large grants of land from the Crown, which they located in the colony of Virginia. At one time the whole county of York, Virginia, was owned by the Powells.*
>
> *William and Nathaniel were both officers in the English Army. They came with Captain John Smith to the English possessions in America, and settled Jamestown in 1607, the first permanent settlement. William Powell was one of the Incorporators of the 2nd Virginia Charter in 1607.*
>
> *The name of Captain Nathaniel Powell is one of the most prominent in Captain John Smith's History. In 1618 Captain Nathaniel Powell was Governor of Virginia for a short time. He was appointed a member of*

the council in 1621. Nathaniel married Miss Tracy, daughter of William Tracy, and granddaughter of Sir John Tracy. The family was massacred by Opechancanough, at Powell's Brooke, on 22 March 1622, near Flowerdew Hundred, on Nathaniel's plantation. Twelve in all were massacred. The Natives "haggled their bodies, and cut off Nathaniel's head to express their utmost height of scorn and cruelty."

William Powell was a member of the Virginia House of Burgesses in 1619. Shortly after the massacre in 1622, Sir George Yeardly, Capt. William Powell, and Captain Richard Butler each took a company and joined forces to avenge the deaths of their friends and relatives. They destroyed everything they could find, and returned to Jamestown, where they stayed a month, quartered at Kecoughtan.

Capt. William Powell and all of his family are believed to have perished in a conflict with a local Native tribe in 1623. Because no heir appeared to inherit the estate, his lands were returned to Governor Berkley, who deeded it to Captain Henry Bishop in 1646.

In 1626, Thomas Powell, (the eldest brother of Nathaniel) and his brothers and sisters then living in England, petitioned the government in regard to William's estate; they stated that William Powell, who had gotten possession of all of Nathaniel's estate in Virginia, was no relation. How they decided this is not recorded, but in 1653 George, Richard and Maud Powell, supposed to have been niece and nephews of Nathaniel, petitioned for the property, which would indicate that Nathaniel and William left no will.

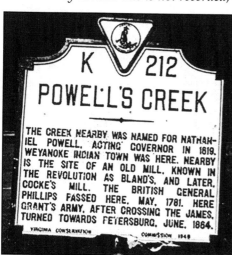

While the Powells seem to have had some wealth, there isn't much consensus among researchers as to their origins in England. There were Powells (or ap Howells) in Brecon, Powys, Wales, from at least the 11th century, where they constructed Castle Madoc. The site of the original castle is now occupied by a house bearing a datestone of 1588 with the initials of Thomas Powell. This was remodeled in the late 17th century and has 19th century additions.

Provenance

The castle belonged to the Powell family until the 18th century, but there is no evidence that our line of Powells ever lived in the castle. Some believe William was the son of a brewer in Surry, England. Whatever the story, it's likely that most of the Powells could be traced back to the early Powells in Wales. The surname Powell is an anglicized version of the Welsh ap Hywell, or Howell. The name became Powell when it was shortened from "ap Howell," joining the P and dropping the H. The name originates in a dynasty of kings of Wales and Brittany in the 9th and 10th centuries. The House of Tudor is one of the Royal houses of England that descends from them.

Early ancestors of the Powells, the fitz Herberts, owned Blaenllyfni Castle, a privately owned stone castle now in ruins near the village of Bwlch in southern Powys, Wales. It was probably built in the early 13th century. It was captured several times and apparently was never fully repaired afterwards and fell into ruins. The ruins are designated an English Scheduled Ancient Monument.

Early ancestors of the Powells, the fitz Herberts, owned Blaenllyfni Castle, a privately owned stone castle now in ruins near the village of Bwlch in southern Powys, Wales.

The "Second Sons"

People often are surprised that so many early Virginians descend from English aristocracy and the kings and queens of Europe. It's not hard to understand when you know about England's *law of primogeniture* that favored the first sons' inheriting lands and titles in England.

> **PRI·MO·GEN·I·TURE**
> - The state of being the firstborn child.
> - The right of succession belonging to the firstborn child, especially the feudal rule by which the whole real estate is passed to the eldest son.

Primogeniture has important implications for the society and culture of early Virginia. Many of the second or third sons who didn't enter the military or the clergy went out to the colonies to make their fortune. Tidewater Virginia evolved as a society descended from sons of English gentry who inherited land grants or land in Virginia.

These so-called "second sons" formed part of what became the southern elite in America. "As early as 1660 every seat on the ruling Council of Virginia was held by members of five interrelated families," writes British historian John Keegan, "and as late as 1775 every council member was descended from one of the 1660 councilors." It wasn't until the American Revolution that primogeniture laws were repealed in the United States.

William and Robert Black
6th and 5th great-grandfathers, Watson line

Anyone who believes that early colonists were interested only in the riches they hoped to find in Virginia might find their mind changed by this quote from the 1744 journal of William Black:

> *The Beautiful young Lady (the Morning) being Risen from her Bed, and with a Countenance blooming with fresh Youth and Sprightliness . . . hanging on her pouting lips, began to take her early walk over the Eastern Woods, when I Rose from my Bed and pass'd two Hours in writing, the rest of the time till Breakfast I spent with my Fiddle and Flute . . .*

William Black emigrated from Scotland to Virginia in 1732. Clearly he was educated, had poetic inclinations and a romantic soul. In fact, he compared himself to William Shakespeare:

> I have more of what Shakespeare calls the Milk of Human Kind than not to have a particular Pleasure in the Company of the Fair Sex, and I now begin to think it Inseperable from my Constitution, as I have few leisure hours but what I would Devote to the Charms of their Conversation did Opptys offer.

At the time William Black wrote his journal, he must have been about 50 years old and it had been four years since the death of his first wife, Helen Metland. After losing his wife, he had sold their property in North Carolina and was living in Chesterfield County, Virginia, where he was appointed to a commission by Virginia Gov. William Gooch "to unite with those from the Colonies of Pennsylvania & Maryland, to treat with the Iroquois or Six Nations of Indians, in reference to the lands West of the Allegheny Mountains."

At Lancaster, Pennsylvania, on October 25, 1744, he signed as secretary of the Virginia Commission at the Treaty of Lancaster. Other members of the Virginia Commission were Col. Thomas Lee and Col. William Beverley of Chesterfield County, and Col. James Littlepage of New Kent County. As secretary, William Black was responsible for arrangements such as lodging and meals, as well as keeping a record of the journey.

William Black's romantic description of the morning is just one of many journal entries that suggest that he no longer was grieving his wife but instead was very interested in young women he met during his journey to Pennsylvania. The following was his most eloquent of several entries:

> I was not long there before I was Bless'd with the Agreeable Company of Miss Molly, which Seem'd to enter the Room like a Goddess, Smiling and all Cheerful, as I always found her; I am No Painter, Neither do I pretend to any thing that way, yet I cannot pass by this Lady, without giving you a Rough Draught of her. I cannot say that she was a Regular Beauty, but she was Such that few cou'd find any Fault with what Dame Nature had done for her. She was of the Middle Size (which I think is the Stature that best becomes the sex), very well Shap'd: her Eyes were Black, full of Fire, and well Slit, they had something in them Remarkably Languishing, and seem'd to Speak the Softness of a Soul Replete with Goodness, her Eye-brows black and finely Arch'd, her Nose was

well turn'd, and of a Just Bigness, and her Mouth was Neither wide nor very little, with Lips of a fine Red, and when they moved discovered two Rows of Teeth white as Ivory and Regularly well Set; her Forehead round and Smooth, as for her Hair, it was a Shining black, but noways harsh. Her Neck, her Arms, and Hands seem to have been made and fitted for her Face, which was of a Complection made up of the Lilly and the Rose. Such was her Person, and I assure you the Charms of her Mind and Conversation was not less Amiable . . .

He continues on with his description of the charming Miss Molly, but also finds time to tend to his duties as secretary for the commission. In this excerpt from his diary, he describes a dinner he arranged:

This day the Commissioners Agreed to give an Entertainment to his Honour the Governor and other Gentlemen of the City, accordingly I went to Engage a Tavern for the Purpose, and Agreed with the Keeper of the Tavern in Water Street, who was to have a handsome Dinner ready by 2 O'clock in the Afternoon, in the Forenoon an Invitation went to the Intended Guests. At 1 the Commissioners and their Levée [levée en masse?] Repair'd to the Tavern and a little past 2 we sat down to a very Grand Table having upwards of Fifteen Dishes on it at once, which was Succeeded by a very fine Collation, among the many Dishes that made our Dinner was a large Turtle, sent as a present to Governor Thomas from a Gentle man of his Acquaintance living in Providence ; after taking away the Cloath, we had the Table Replenished with all the sorts of Wine the Tavern cou'd afford, and that in great Abundance.

Although the journal contained a few routine details of his travels, the information was in no way as detailed as William Black's descriptions of the people, places and events he experienced. If he kept an official record of the Commission's activities as would be expected of a secretary, it was in a different notebook than this one.

It is interesting that this personal notebook was preserved as a result of the paper shortage during the Revolutionary War. After William Black's death in 1782, his third wife, Frances Carthcart Taylor, married William Claiborne. William Claibourne, needing paper to keep records pertaining to his plantation, turned the notebook over and made use of the blank pages, back to front. This notebook eventually became the property of the Pennsylvania Archives, when the William Claiborne papers came into their possession. (For more information about the Claibornes, see the profile of Robert Coleman, whose mother was Rebecca Claiborne.)

That educated men like William Black prospered in Virginia was a product of the policies of Governor William Berkeley during the late 1600s. Berkeley set out to imitate the society of inequality of wealth and education that he knew in England. To achieve that goal, he recruited from England both younger sons with no inheritance and supporters of the king who were fleeing a civil war. He promoted them to lucrative offices and granted them large estates.

By the 1700s, Virginians began to define themselves by their rural settlement. Slavery freed Virginia's leaders from farming and positioned them to read and theorize, in the manner of the ancients. Until after the American Revolution, they in effect ruled Virginia. The middle and lower class families—the vast majority of the population—have been forgotten.

According to Scottish baptismal records, William Black was born in 1663 in Kilconquhar, Fife, Scotland, the son of James Black and Margrat Cowltrie. James Black is believed to have been a wealthy wool merchant in Aberdeen.

William Black married his first wife, Helen Metland, in 1717, and they lived in Kirkcaldy, Fife, Scotland where they had 11 or 12 children before they traveled to the Virginia colony in about 1735. Helen died at the birth of their last son, James, born in Onslow, North Carolina, in 1740. Our family descends from their son Robert, one of eight of their sons who accompanied them to Virginia.

The surname Black was common in Fife, Edinburgh and Glasgow, Scotland. Many descend from French Huguenots named "Le Noir," who migrated to Ireland from France to escape religious persecution in 1642, according to John O'Hart's book, *Irish Pedigrees*. They became naturalized and had their name anglicized to Black. Shortly after the Blacks fought with the English during the 17th century's Cromwellian war in Ireland, they migrated to Scotland, perhaps due to the unrest among Irish Nationalists who were bitter about the English colonization of Ireland.

William and Mary Bostick
8th great-grandfather, 7th great-grandmother, Watson line

William Bostick and his 14-year-old daughter, Mary, arrived in Virginia in about 1684, the year that records show Mary married William Leake. Mary and William Leake settled in Rocky Springs, Goochland, Virginia, where they had at least eight children. Apparently Mary's mother died, either in England or on the passage over to Virginia. Mary wrote in her family bible: "We have been in America one year May 25th 1686; Mary Bostick, her Booke, given by her grandfather."

William Bostick's father was Charles Bostick. As far as I can tell, Charles never came to Virginia. However, just to confuse matters, there was a Charles Bostick who did go to Virginia before William and Mary arrived. This Charles also had a son named William. The similar family names would suggest that the families might be related.

Bostick descendants went to South Carolina and developed Bostick Plantation which had more than 70,000 acres. The family is one of fewer than 200 families who still hold title to an original land grant from King George III, now about 5,000 acres. The original plantation house was burned during the Civil War. The reconstructed plantation house and property had been used for hunting but now is being sold.

William and Mary Bostick came from Nottinghamshire, England, but they descend from Bosticks from the town of Bostock in Cheshire, England. The original spelling of the town's name was Botestoch, and it was run by the Saxon lord, Osmer, until the Norman's took over the town in 1070. *The Domesday Book,* an inventory of all the properties in the kingdom ordered by William the Conqueror in 1086, describes much of Cheshire to have been wasted and depopulated by the Norman Conquest. It informs us that Osmer had been holder of the manor of Bostock before it fell to the new Norman owner, Richard de Vernon. The Bostocks were tenants of the Vernon family.

We know that surnames were not used until after the Norman Conquest, when the king required taxes from all residents and needed family names to identify them. The Bostick (or Bostock) surname was taken from the name of the town, using the familiar Norman "de" (of) to

Nine generations of Bostocks were lords of the manor of Bostock until 1489 when the title fell to other families. The current Bostock House was rebuilt in 1775.

create the name de Bostick. An original family pedigree of the Bostock lords created during the Middle Ages claims descent from Osmer, the Saxon lord.

The Bostock family continued as lords of the manor through nine generations until William de Bostick died childless in 1489 and the manor fell into the hands of his sister Anne's husband, Sir John Savage. By 1580, a list of Cheshire land owners included only one Bostock, Henry, who resided at Bostock Old Hall. Any other Bostocks still in the area were working for Henry Bostock or the Savages. This might explain why this once noble family would join the rush to acquire land in the colonies.

The current Bostock Hall, now called Bostock House, is a country house to the northeast of Winsford, Cheshire, England. It was rebuilt in 1775 by Edward Tomkinson. The house is recorded in the National Heritage List for England as a designated Grade II listed building.

Giles Carter
8th great-grandfather, Walker line

I don't know the source of this quote, but it certainly describes the life of our immigrant ancestor, Giles Carter of Virginia:

> *One fact that sets Giles apart is that throughout his life people gave him things. These were not small gifts: he received cows and pigs, tons of tobacco, houses, and the full use of an entire plantation . . . I don't know what it was about Giles Carter that inspired so much generosity in people.*

Giles Carter came to Virginia in 1653 with a group of fifteen persons whose passage provided a headright of 750 acres to William Fry for sponsoring their passage. Headrights were legal grants of 50 acres of land to support expansion of the population of the colonies. While some of these people may have been family members, most were indentured servants who would have agreed to work a few years to pay for their passage then receive land and other property to live independently.

Giles Carter was not typical of most servants, however, in that the Carter family of Gloucestershire descended from royalty. Giles' "indenture" may actually have been part of a strategy for wealthy landowners to add to their land holdings by listing any new arrivals to Virginia as indentures.

The fact that Giles Carter was different from most servants is illustrated by the preferential treatment he received from several Virginia landowners. Soon after his arrival, John Rowen awarded to Giles in his will a cow and the use for one year of a house and land on Rowen's Turkey Island plantation.

While he was living on Rowen's plantation he became associated with James Crewes, a member of the House of Burgesses and a merchant dealing in tobacco and furs in Virginia and England. Giles married Crewes' daughter, Hannah, and the Carter family lived on Crewes' 500-acre plantation at Turkey Island after leaving the Rowen plantation.

In 1676, James Crewes left nearly all of his estate to the family of Giles Carter. Crewes wrote in his will, "It is my desire that my loving friend Giles Carter should live here in my said house and command my servants and make crops or any other thing as shall be convenient and necessary for the said plantation, and so to give an account yearly if my said executor shall order. Giles was required to pay rent to the estate in the amount of one grain of corn each year."

William Randolph purchased a portion of his Turkey Island property from Giles Carter.

Some of James Crewes' relatives refused to accept the terms of his will and sold their 500 acres of the Turkey Island plantation to William Randolph. Randolph paid them "three acres and 15 pounds of lawful money of England," but paid 20 pounds to Giles Carter for the 60 acres Giles had received as a gift from James Crewes.

Giles appears frequently in the record books of Henrico County. He never sought public office or gained a prestigious name in commerce or the military, but he seemed always to have been available in his Turkey Island neighborhood to perform jury service, witness a will or a deed, appraise an estate, or to win 500 pounds of tobacco in a dice game.

Giles Carter continued to expand his holdings during his lifetime, including adding 800 acres for transporting 16 persons. Giles' will left most of his estate to his wife, Hannah, and his youngest son, Giles. He had given land to his six other children before his death.

Descendants of the immigrant Giles Carter of Henrico County have disagreed for centuries over who were his parents. The confusion comes about because there actually were two Giles Carters who went to Virginia in the early 1600s. The first visit in 1620 is described in a book by Gen. William Harding Carter,

> *The first Giles Carter of whom there is any record in Virginia, came from Gloucestershire, England, with William Tracey on the Supply, which sailed from Bristol, September 24th, 1620 and arrived at Berkley January 29th, 1620. After looking over the situation Giles Carter returned to England immediately before or just after the Indian massacre of Friday, April 1st, 1622. The Carter family of Goucestershire, England, in which Gyles or Giles appears as a Christian name, was connected with the Tracey family by the marriage of Gyles Carter and Elizabeth Tracey. This Giles was a son of John Carter of Lower Sewell, who was High Sheriff of Gloucester in 1612.*

While most researchers believe that the first Giles Carter was the father of our ancestor, Giles Carter of Henrico County, genealogist Richard Zeiman has made it his quest to disprove and erase this historical inaccuracy. Zeiman's research has failed to convince most Carter researchers, though, who continue to show Giles 1634 as the son of Giles 1604. The reason is that the older Giles married Elizabeth Tracy whose family ties have been traced to royal lines that extend back to the Norman Conquest of 1066.

I agree with Zeiman and others, however, that while the two Giles Carters may be related, Giles 1634 probably did not share the royal lines of the Tracy family. Another Carter researcher, Joy Carter Johnstone, offers as proof that Giles 1604 could not have been the father by citing a plaque she found in a church in Cold Aston, Glouchestershire:

> Anno Dom 1664 – Giles Carter the eldest son of John Carter of Netherswell Co. of Gloucester, Esq. his two brothers being John Carter of Charlton Abbots and William Carter of Bressnorton in Oxford married Elizabeth the daughter of Paul Tracye of Standwell and died without issue.

Joy Johnstone and Zeiman believe that the father of Giles Carter of Henrico County was Theodore Carter who, according to parish records of Cirenchester, Gloucestershire, England, had a son Giles born in 1634 and christened April 24, 1635. That birth date coincides with Giles' 1680 deposition, in which he declares himself to be 46 years old. Also, our Giles Carter named his first son Theodrick.

The surname Carter is common in the United States. Perhaps the most notable Carter was our 39th president, Jimmy Carter. If anyone should carry the flag for our Carter ancestors, I'm glad it's this man. He rose from being a peanut farmer in Georgia to leading the nation. After his presidency, he did more to lead by example in helping the poor and promoting world peace than any other former president.

Thomas and William Peter Christian

Our immigrant ancestors Thomas and Peter Christian share the same last name and roots in the Isle of Man and probably are related. The Isle of Man is a tiny island—just 221 square miles—located in the Irish sea between England and Ireland. According to family legend, the Christian family, one of the oldest and most distinguished on the island, descended from Giolla Chríost, or Christian in Gaelic,

an 11th century associate of the Viking king, Godred Crovan, who established the Kingdom of Mann and conquered Dublin.

Thomas Christian
8th great-grandfather, Watson line
Thomas Christian, an emigrant from the Isle of Man, probably arrived in Virginia in 1657, when he claimed his first land there. In 1663, he married another emigrant from Man, Elinor Kewley, and together they had about 11 children. He and his children continued to acquire land until they held several large plantations in Charles City County.

Green Oak Farm, Thomas Christian's farm, was originally called "Cherry Bottom." The main dwelling house was built sometime between 1657 and 1687 and is considered to be one of the oldest houses in Virginia. The nails and brick from the chimney were brought over from England and paid for with tobacco. The wings which are now part of the main house originally were built on the back of the house. According to an 1897 article, Green Oak Farm is the only known property in Virginia that has been passed to future generations through will only since the original patent. It has never been deeded. The property has been in the Christian family name since 1657. The home is not open to the public but can be viewed at 11400 Green Oak Road, Charles City, Virginia.

The 18th and 19th centuries produced many distinguished descendants of the immigrant Thomas Christian. Following the precedent set by their judicial ancestors on the Isle of Man, at least seven Christian family members held the position of clerk of the courts for Virginia counties and cities. Two others were judges and at least four became doctors.

Capt. Henry Christian served in the American Army of the Revolutionary War under Major General Marquis de Lafayette. Robert Christian, whose home, Cedar Grove in New Kent County, now is listed in the National Register of Historic Places, was colonel in the Virginia Militia and a member of the General Assembly of Virginia. His daughter, Letitia Christian, was the first wife of President John Tyler.

By the time of the Civil War, five or six generations of Christians had multiplied and spread to nearly every state in the union. Nearly 600 Christian family members fought in the Confederate Army and another

Green Oak Farm in Charles City, Virginia, has been owned by the Christian family since the 1600s.

400 defended the Union. African Americans (designated U.S. Colored troops) supporting the Union included 64 with the surname Christian—probably former slaves from Christian family plantations.

Thomas Christian has ties to both our Watson and Walker family lines through the marriage of his son Thomas II to Rebecca New, the granddaughter of Agnes Barrett and Richard New. Rebecca's sister Elizabeth married Walker ancestor John Tuley. Several early Virginia documents confirm the link between the Christians and the Tuleys. Martha, the daughter of Thomas I, married Watson ancestor John Mask, so the family has ties to the immigrant Mask and Leake families as well.

William Christian led the Manx Rebellion of 1651 against English rulers.

Many believe Thomas Christian was a son of the famous Isle of Man dissident William Christian. The Christian family attained an important position in the Isle of Man at an early date. In the 15th century, John McChristen II was Deemster of the Isle of Man and Justiciarus Regis—a judge appointed by the king of England. Members of the McChristen/McChristian/Christian family continued to serve as judges in the Isle of Man until the 1600s. William Christian was appointed receiver general, in command of the island militia.

William Christian staged a revolt, known as the Manx Rebellion of 1651, against acts instituted by English rulers. Following the rebellion, he became legendary as Illiam Dhône or "Brown William" for his dark hair. William remained receiver general and became governor of the Isle of Man in 1656. Two years later, however, he was accused of misappropriating money, although these charges were never substantiated. He fled to England, and in 1660 was arrested in London.

After serving a year of imprisonment, William returned to Man, hoping that his offence against the English Lord of Man would be condoned under the Act of Indemnity of 1661. However, he was ordered seized and brought to trial. At his trial, William refused to plead and a packed House of Keys declared that his life and property were at the mercy of the Lord of Man. The Deemsters then passed sentence, and William Christian was executed by shooting in 1663.

William Christian was immortalized in the Manx ballad "Baase Illiam Dhône," which was translated into English by John Crellin in 1774 and through the references to him in Sir Walter Scott's "Peveril of the Peak."

Milntown Estate was the Christian family home from the early 1500s when the property was acquired by John McCrysten III. It is located in the parish of Lazayre near Ramsey, Isle of Man.

According to an unknown source, probably oral history,

> *By the time of William Christian's execution, the family had acquired Ewanrigg Hall in Cumberland, North West England. For the next 150 years they lived there and leased Milntown, their estate on Isle of Man, to tenants. Marrying into the Curwen family of Workington Hall their fortunes were once again in the ascendancy and Ewan Christian was the only person ever to have been both an MP in the House of Commons and a Member of the Isle of Man's House of Keys. It was also during this time that Fletcher Christian, a member of one of the branches of the family, reached notoriety as the head of the mutineers on HMS Bounty. The family returned to enlarge and refurbish Milntown in 1830.*

Clockwise from upper left: Workington Hall, Ewanrigg Hall and Milntown Estate. Milntown Estate was the Christian family home from the early 1500s. Ewanrigg Hall, the Christian family home in Cumberland, England, burned in 2015. The Christian family gained Workington Hall through marriage. It was destroyed during World War II.

William Bell Christian was the last to own Milntown but sadly was bankrupt on his death in 1886. His widow, son and two daughters rented the estate from the administrators and his son Edward was the last Christian to die at Milntown in 1915.

Today the Milntown house and gardens are open at certain times for house tours. Three apartments are available for weekly rental and the Milntown Cafe serves breakfast, lunch and afternoon tea. Ewanrigg Hall was destroyed by fire in 2015 and the property was sold for development. The ruins of Workington Hall, which burned during World War II, can be seen on the outskirts of the town of Workington in Cumbria.

William Peter Christian
2nd great-grandfather, Watson line

Our immigrant ancestors are a diverse and interesting lot, but Peter Christian takes the prize for most colorful. My grandmother told us he was a famous sea captain. This story recalled by his son, Zene Christian, probably describes his life at sea more accurately:

Peter and his uncle were sailors on a privateer. As a result of carelessness in choice of ships they preyed on [i.e., ships of the British trade], the English Crown put a price on their head and they were forced to leave England and the sea. They entered the U.S. either at the port of Mobile, Alabama, or of Gulfport, Mississippi.

Another descendant's account claims that "Peter's mother and father died when Pete was 13 years old. He worked on a ship for 30 years. Came back to London, married Margaret Turner and stayed in London two years. They had two children, Mary and Margaret Christian. He left London and came to Mobile, Alabama . . ."

Tracing Peter's history tends to leave me shaking my head. After years of research, I still don't know for sure when he was born, when he arrived in the United States, how many wives he had, or even the year of his death. I'm not even sure his name was William Peter—most of his descendants call him Peter. Family members and U.S. census reports have variously identified his place of birth as the Isle of Man, London and Liverpool, England. His year of birth may have been 1786, 1800, 1810, 1815 or 1816, and his year of death may have been 1874, 1875 or 1878.

I have to assume that he arrived in the U.S. sometime before 1840. His daughter Mary Jane Christian was born in 1844 in Arkansas, and there is a Wm. Christian recorded in the 1840 Richland, Phillips, Arkansas, census living with one adult and three children. It's possible that the Margaret Turner he married in London joined him there with their children.

Peter married Susan Turner (a relative of Margaret's perhaps?) from Tennessee in about 1846. The couple lived in Mississippi and raised five children there between 1847 and 1858, including my great-grandfather, George Bartley Christian. In about 1860, Peter married Polly Waldon and had seven more children with her.

Peter Christian would have been about 46 years old at the start of the Civil War in 1861, depending on what source you choose to believe regarding his birth date. One of his granddaughters said that she heard that Peter had served in the Confederate Army during the war but the record is unclear. A Peter Christian was listed among Confederate recruits from Louisiana; his record shows that he served as a private in "4 Regiment, 3 Brigade, 1 Division, Louisiana Militia, Company E."

Peter Christian's family lived in Bryan's Mill, Texas, until about 1920, when some of them moved to Arizona.

It is possible that Peter Christian was recruited or volunteered in Louisiana, but according to the 1860 census, he was living in Cherry Hill, Calhoun Co., Mississippi, with his wife "Mary," presumed to be the widow Polley A. Waldron from Alabama, whom he married in 1860. According to another descendant, "Pete left Corinth, Mississippi, just before the Civil War. He went to Arkansas and filed on land where Blackton, Arkansas, now is."

By 1870, Peter Christian and his family were living in Titus, Texas. Polley is believed to have died in that year, possibly at the birth of her son, William Peter. Peter may have married again, after Polley's death, to Elizabeth Long in 1873. Peter died sometime between 1874 and 1878 in Bryan's Mill, Cass County. He was buried in nearby Douglasville.

John Coffey
8th great-grandfather, Watson line

John Coffey came to Virginia in 1637. He probably emigrated from County Cork, Ireland, as an indentured servant to Nicholas Hill.

He married an English immigrant named Mary Jolliffe during the 1640s. Mary may have been among the many "mail-order brides" delivered to the colonies in the early 1600s. Men in the colonies vastly outnumbered women so ships were sent to the colonies with only women aboard to provide wives for them. The women who signed up to leave England for Jamestown were offered substantial incentives. They were provided a dowry of clothing, linens, and other furnishings, free transportation to the colony, and even a plot of land. They were also promised their pick of wealthy husbands and provided with food and shelter while they made their decision.

John Coffey and Mary Jolliffe had at least four sons between 1648 and 1670. Our direct family line to the Coffey name continued through four generations in Virginia until Mildred Coffey married Samuel Coleman in 1785 and moved to Kentucky.

The Coffey family has maintained a low profile since settling in colonial Virginia, but their ancestors had a major impact on early Ireland. The name Coffey originally was "Cobhthaigh," a name that originates from Celtic bands that invaded and occupied Ireland. The Cobhthaigh line is traced back to Olbol Flann Beag, king of Munster, and to brothers Ithe and Bile, relatives to Milesius, king of Spain.

In the 9th century, Fergus Mos O'Cobhthaigh brought the leaders of the three most warring clans of Ireland, the O'Briens, O'Neils, and

In the 9th century, Coffey ancestor Fergus Mos O'Cobhthaigh brought leaders of warring clans of Ireland together at Tara to sign a peace treaty. The Mound of the Hostages at Tara dates to about 2500 BC.

McCarthys together at Tara where a peace treaty was signed. The Hill of Tara was once the ancient seat of power in Ireland—142 kings are said to have reigned there in prehistoric and historic times. For Fergus Mos O'Cobhthaigh's diplomacy and respect for law and order, he was made the supreme judge of Eire, a highly respected position which was held by the family for seven generations.

John Coffey is believed to be the son of Hugh Coffee of Cork, born in 1594. Hugh was married to Agnes Elizabeth Montgomery, whose family were Normans who immigrated to England from Calvados, Normandy. Clan Montgomery settled along the border between Wales and England, then immigrated to Scotland in the 12th century with the FitzAlans.

Through marriage, the Montgomery Clan acquired the Eglinton Castle in Eaglesham, Renfrewshire. The castle was burned and Hugh Montgomery, the 4th Earl of Eglinton, was murdered during ongoing battles between the Montgomerys and Cunninghams in the 15th and 16th centuries.

A bloody revenge swept over Cunninghams with Montgomerys killing every Cunningham they found. King James VI of Scotland eventually made the chiefs of the two clans shake hands. In 1661, William Cunningham, 9th Earl of Glencairn, married Margaret Montgomery, daughter of Alexander, 6th Earl of Eglinton, bringing an end to the feud. A branch of Scottish Montgomerys settled in Donegal, Ireland, in 1628.

John Montgomery, an ancestor of the Earls of Eglington, married Agnes MacDonald, whose mother was Margaret Stewart, daughter of Scottish King Robert II Stewart. His father was Walter Stewart, 6th High Steward of Scotland, and his mother was Marjorie Bruce, daughter of the first King Robert de Brus of Scotland. We directly descend from Marjorie

A 19th century painting of the ruins of Turnbury Castle, Ayrshire, birthplace of Robert de Brus.

Bruce and a long line of Roberts who ruled Scotland in various capacities, including:

Robert I "Robert de Brus (Bruce)," King of Scotland 1306-1329:
Ruling for 23 years, Robert is best known for fighting both Edward I and Edward II of England and uniting both the Highlands and Lowlands in battles for Scottish independence. Robert I was born at Turnberry Castle, Ayrshire, the home of his mother, Marjorie Bruce. Robert de Brus ordered the destruction of the castle in 1310 to prevent it from falling to the English. Today, the castle ruins are surrounded on three sides by the sea and on the landward side, Trump Turnberry Golf Course. The body of Robert I was interred at Dunfermline Abbey in Dunfermline, Fife, and his heart at Melrose Abbey in Melrose, Roxburghshire. Dunfermline Abbey, founded in 1128, is now a Church of Scotland parish church and is open to the public. Melrose Abbey was founded in 1136, disestablished in 1609 and now is in partial ruins. The grounds and museum are open to the public.

The body of Robert de Brus was interred at Melrose Abbey (left) and Dunfermline Abbey.

Robert II, King of Scotland 1371–1390:
Robert II was the first of the Royal House of Stewart/Stuart. He died in Dundonald Castle, Ayshire, which is open to the public. His burial place, Scone Abbey, was damaged in 1559 by a mob during the Reformation. Scone Palace, built in the 19th century, stands on the grounds of the original abbey which was one of Scotland's most revered historic sites. It is open to the public.

Seven Lords of Annandale named Robert de Brus, 1124 to 1332:
The Lord of Annandale was a lordship in southern Scotland established by David I of Scotland for his friend Robert de Brus. Our ancestry through Robert de Brus includes Earls of Pembroke Richard (Strongbow) de Clare and William Marshal, and Henry III of England.

Robert Coleman
8th great-grandfather, Watson line

Robert Coleman wasn't a wealthy man when he arrived in Virginia in 1637 but at one time his family was one of the most prosperous in England. Because of their wealth and influence, Coleman men attracted and married women who were direct descendants of nobles and royals from across Europe.

The Colemans were from Brent Eleigh, a village near Lavenham in the southwest corner of Suffolk, England, an area that had long been famous for its cloth production. Like most of the major families in the area, the Colemans made their money from the wool trade in the 15th and 16th centuries. Lavenham was known especially for its blue broadcloth.

By the late 15th century, the town was among the richest in the British Isles. The town's prosperity at this time can be seen in the lavishly constructed wool church of St. Peter and St. Paul, which stands on a hilltop at the end of the main high street. The church, completed in 1525, is excessively large for the size of the village. With a tower standing 141 feet high, it lays claim to being the highest village church tower in Britain.

The Coleman family built St. Peter and St. Paul Church in Lavenham, which claims to have the highest village church tower in Britain.

Edward Coleman, Robert's great-grandfather, had established himself as one of the wealthiest wool merchants during the 1550s. At about the same time, Lavenham's industry was badly affected by the sale of cloth made by Dutch refugees settled in Colchester that was cheaper, lighter and more fashionable than that made in Lavenham. Cheaper imports from Europe also contributed to the village's decline, and by 1600 it no longer was a major trading town.

All was not lost for the Colemans, however, for the family had invested their fortune in land. In 1607, Edward Coleman's younger son, Samuel, bought the manors of Brent Eleigh and Fennhall from Sir Robert Jermyn of Rushbrooke.

Today, the Coleman's hometown, Lavenham, often is described as England's finest and most perfect surviving medieval village. The sudden and dramatic change to the town's fortune is the principal reason more than 300 medieval and Tudor buildings have changed very little since the late 1500s. Descendants of Edward Coleman and the other wealthy wool merchants could not afford to modernize and rebuild. The village has been used as a location for films by John Lennon and Yoko Ono and Stanley Kubrick, and most recently for scenes from *Harry Potter and the Deathly Hallows*.

It was land that brought Robert Coleman to Virginia, along with three of his brothers, all sons of Richard Coleman and Rebecca Claiborne. There was another Robert Coleman in Virginia around the same time as our Robert, so our Robert has been distinguished as the "Mobjack Bay" Robert for his property located on Mobjack Bay in Abingdon Parish, Gloucester County.

The Abingdon Parish Register was destroyed in 1676, so little is known about Robert's life in Virginia. He married Elizabeth Grizzell who may have immigrated to Virginia or may have been born after the arrival of her father and grandfather, both named William Grizzell. For some reason, her parents and grandfather all are recorded to have died in 1636. I don't know if that was due simply to loss of records, if they were killed in an attack by Natives, or more likely died from one of the diseases that frequented the colony.

Althorp House in Northamptonshire has been the family seat of the Spencer family for more than 500 years.

Quierzy Castle, where Charles Martel died in 741, was rebuilt in the 15th century.

Robert and Elizabeth Coleman had six known surviving children. His eldest son, Thomas, born before 1654, would have inherited most of his father's Gloucester County land, as was the custom in England and in the colonies in the early years. He and his wife Rebecca Claiborne left many descendants who settled in Virginia and points west.

Through our Coleman ancestors, we have direct links to some of the most powerful leaders in early Europe. I have traced them back to the 3rd century, revealing direct lines to rulers of the Franks, Visogoths, the Plantagenet and to Charlemagne, Emperor of the Roman Empire in the 9th century, who united most of Europe for a time.

The Coleman's wealth during the 14th and 15th centuries must have made them attractive suitors to members of England's nobility. Robert Coleman's grandmother was Mary Spencer who married James Coleman in about 1600. The Spencer family today is one of Britain's most aristocratic families. Sir Winston Churchill and Diana, Princess of Wales, were among the most prominent family members of the 20th century. The family descends from the de Spencers, the House of Stuart (see John Coffey profile for list of Stuart rulers), the Bourbons, the Medicis, the Wittelsbachs, the Hanovers, the Sforzas, the Habsburgs, and the Houses of Howard and Boleyn through Mary Boleyn, Mistress of Henry VIII of England.

The Basilica of St. Denis, St. Denis, France, where nearly every French king from the 10th to the 18th centuries was buried.

Aachen Cathedral in Western Germany and Charlemagne's throne in the Palatine Chapel of the cathedral.

Mary Spencer ancestry: The Spencers rose to prominence in England in the 16th century through prudent investment in property and farming, especially raising sheep. During a debate in the House of Lords, Sir Robert Spencer was speaking about something that their great ancestors had done when suddenly the Earl of Arundel, whose family had held peerages since the 13th century, cut him off and said "My Lord, when these things you speak of were doing, your ancestors were keeping sheep." Lord Spencer then instantly replied, "When my ancestors as you say were keeping sheep, your ancestors were plotting treason."

Althorp House in Northamptonshire has been the family seat of the Spencer family for more than 500 years. The 90-room Tudor mansion sits on a 13,000-acre estate. The estate and house are open to the public during the summer months.

Count Fulk IV was born in Angers, France, probably at Chateau d'Angers, a castle founded in the 9th century.

Many of Charlamagne's family are buried at the Abbey of Saint-Arnould in Metz, France.

The Spencers' original estate, Wormleighton Manor in Warsickshire was burned down in 1645 during the English Civil War. Today, all that is left of the manor, which was once four times the size of Althorp, is the Wormleighton Manor Gatehouse and Tower Cottage which is a Grade II listed building, and the northern range of the manor.

Because Robert de Spencer married Lady Eleanor Beaufort in the 15th century, our family directly descends from kings of England and France, and emperors of the Roman Empire. Here are some of the members of Medieval European nobility from whom we descend:

7th century

Charles Martel, Duke and Prince of the Franks:
Skilled as an administrator as well as a warrior, Charles is considered to be a founding figure of the European Middle Ages. He was born in Herstal, Belgium, in 686 and died at the Château de Quierzy. Quierzy Castle was rebuilt in the 15th century as the fortress of the bishops of Noyon and opens to the public for special events. He is buried in the Basilica of St. Denis, St. Denis, France.

8th century

Pepin the Short, King of the Franks, Carolingian:
Pepin reigned over Francia jointly with his elder brother Carloman. Pepin ruled in Neustria, Burgundy, and Provence, while his brother established himself in Austrasia, Alemannia and Thuringia. Pepin and his wife Bertrada are both interred in the Basilica of Saint Denis, along with most of the French kings.

Charlemagne, or Charles the Great, King of the Franks, King of the Lombards, Emperor of the Romans:
He has been called the "Father of Europe" as he united most of Western Europe during the early Middle Ages. He embarked on a mission to unite all Germanic peoples into one kingdom, and convert his subjects to Christianity. He had 18 children with eight of his ten known wives or concubines, another reason he might be known as the "Father of Europe." Charlemagne died in the Palace of Aachen in western Germany.

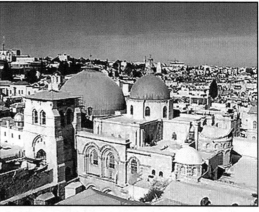

Several French kings were crowned at Reims Cathedral, Paris (left). Count Fulk IV was buried at the Church of the Holy Sepulchre in Jerusalem (above).

Today much of the palace has been destroyed, but the Palatine Chapel in the Cathedral of Aachen has been preserved and is considered a masterpiece of Carolingian architecture. The cathedral is open to the public after daily services and guided tours are available.

Louis I the Pious, King of Franks, King of Aquitaine, and co-Emperor of the Roman Empire with his father, Charlemagne:
Louis was born in Villa Cassinogilum in Aquitaine, France, where his mother, Hildegard of Vinzgouw, was staying while his father Charlemagne was on campaign in Spain. The villa was located in what now is Chasseneuil-du-Poitou in the Aquitaine region of France. After trying to split the kingdom among his sons, Louis I ended up fighting three civil wars with his three sons by his first wife when they resisted his attempts to give power to his son by his second wife. While in Aquitaine he was able to expand the kingdom into Spain by defeating the Muslims. He died in the Ingelheim Imperial Palace in the Rhineland-Palatinate, Germany. There is a museum and tours that include remnants of the Imperial Palace in Ingelheim. Louis I is buried in the Abbey of Saint-Arnould in Metz, the burial place of many of Charlemagne's family, which is open to the public.

9th century

Charles the Bald, King of West Francia and Italy, and Roman Emperor:
After a series of civil wars during the reign of his father, Louis the Pious, Charles succeeded by the Treaty of Verdun in acquiring the western third of the Carolingian Empire. He may have been nicknamed "The Bald" not because he was bald but

King Louis VII was crowned in 1137 at Bourges Cathedral, Bourges, France (above). King Alfonso VIII was buried in the Abbey of Santa María la Real de Las Huelgas in Burgos, Spain.

because he was very hairy. Charles was born in the Palace at Aachen in what now is Aachen, Germany. He died while trying to cross the Alps at Mont Cenis Pass and is buried in the Basilica of St. Denis.

12th century

Fulk IV, Count of Anjou, King of Jerusalem, Plantagenet:
Fulk ruled as Count of Anjou and then as joint ruler of Jerusalem with King Baldwin II of Jerusalem. Fulk was born in Angers, France, probably at Chateau d'Angers, a castle founded in the 9th century and expanded in the 13th century. The castle now is open to the public as a museum. He died in a hunting accident in Acre, Jerusalem, and was buried at the Church of the Holy Sepulchre in Jerusalem. The church, now a favorite tourist site, was consecrated in 335 and completed in 1048 by Emperor Constantine IX.

Louis VII, King of the Franks, "the Younger," Capet:
Louis was born in Paris and ruled for 43 years. He was crowned twice, first at Reims Cathedral in 1131 and in Bourges in 1137. Both cathedrals are prime examples of Gothic architecture and are open to the public. Louis VII's reign saw the founding of the University of Paris and the disastrous Second Crusade. He is buried in the Cathedral of St. Denis.

Clockwise from left, places in France connected with the life of Henry II, King of England: Fontevraud Abbey, Chateau de Chinon and the Palace of the Counts of Maine in Le Mans.

Alfonso VIII, King of Castile and Toledo:
Alfonso was proclaimed king at the age of two, leaving his kingdom in disorder. At age 15, he came forth to restore order and continued to rule for another 41 years. He married Eleanor Plantagenet, daughter of Henry II, King of England. In Soria, where Alfonso was born, remains of the castle and other 12th century buildings are open to the public. He died in Gutierre-Munoz and is buried in the Abbey of Santa María la Real de Las Huelgas in Burgos, Spain, founded in 1187, which is open to the public.

Louis VIII, King of France, "the Lion" Capet:
Louis was King of France for only three years, and claimed the title of King of England for one year after an invasion of southern England. The coronation of Louis VIII took place in the Reims Cathedral, which is open to the public. He died from illness in 1226 and is buried at the Basilica of St. Denis.

Philip II, King of France, "Philip Augustus":
Phillip ruled for 43 years, transforming France from a small feudal state into the most prosperous and powerful country in Europe. He was born

Clockwise from right: Worcester Cathedral and Newark Castle in Nottinghamshire are connected to the life of King John of England. Le Mans Cathedral in France is the site of Geoffrey Plantagenet's burial.

in Gonesse, France, and crowned at Reims Cathedral at age 14. He died at Mantes-la-Joiie and was interred in the Basilica of St. Denis.

Henry II, King of England, Plantagenet:
Henry ruled as Count of Anjou, Count of Maine, Duke of Normandy, Duke of Aquitaine, Count of Nantes and Lord of Ireland at various times; he also controlled Wales, Scotland and Brittany. He was born in the Palace of the Counts of Maine in Le Mans France, which today is the town hall of Le Mans and open to the public. He died at the Chateau de Chinon, France, and is buried at Fontevraud Abbey, France, both also open to the public.

Geoffrey Plantagenet, Count of Anjou:
Geoffrey was count of Anjou, Touraine, and Maine by inheritance from 1129 and then Duke of Normandy by conquest from 1144. The name "Plantagenet" was taken from the yellow broom flowers (planta genista) he wore on his helmet. The rule of three kings of England, Geoffrey's son Henry II and grandsons Richard and John, was known as the Angevin Empire for their origins in Anjou, France. Geoffrey was born in Anjou and died in Chateau-du-Loir. He was buried at Le Mans Cathedral, Le Mans, which is open to the public.

John, King of England, Plantagenet: John, who ruled for 17 years, was known as "John Lackland" because he lost the duchy of Normandy to the King of France, resulting in the collapse of most of the Angevin Empire. He was born at Beaumont Palace, Oxford, died at Newark Castle, Newark-on-Trent, Nottinghamshire, and was buried at

Clockwise from top left: Chateau de Vincennes near Paris; Cathedral of Monreale near Palermo, Italy; Palace of Fontainebleu, France.

Worchester Cathedral. Newark Castle and Worchester Cathedral are open to the public.

12th century

Louis IX, King of France, "Saint Louis" Capet:
He was crowned King of France at age 12, although his mother, Blanche of Castile, ruled as regent until he reached maturity. He was born in Poissy, France, and lived at the Palace of Fontainebleu. He went on three crusades during his 50-year reign, dying of illness on the last in Tunis. He was the only French king to be declared a saint. His heart is buried in the Norman Cathedral of Monreale near Palermo, Italy, and his bones are interred at the Basilica of St. Denis. All of these sites are open to the public.

Philip IV, King of France and Navarre:
During the 13th century, Philip inherited the crown of France from his father, Philip III, and became King of Navarre (Basque Spain) by virtue of his wife, Joan of Navarre. His children include Charles IV of France, Louis X of France, Philip V of France and Isabella of France. Princes from his house ruled Naples and Hungary. He was born and died in the Palace of Fontainebleu, now a favorite tourist attraction near Paris, and is buried at the Basilica of St. Denis near Paris.

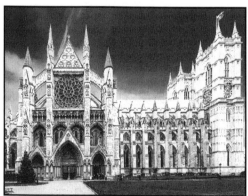

Joan of Navarre, Queen of Navarre and France, and Countess of Champagne:
In the 13th century, Joan was directly active as countess of Champaign, which, while being a county rather than a kingdom, was much richer and more strategically important than Navarre. Joan was

Westminster Abbey (above) is the traditional place of coronation and burial site for English monarchs. and the Palace of Westminster, London, was a royal residence since the 11th century.

born in Bar-sur-Seine, France, which was destroyed by England in 1359 and suffered greatly in the religious wars of the 16th century. She died at the Chateau de Vincennes near Paris, which is open for visits and tours; she is buried in the Basilica of St. Denis.

Philip III, King of France:
Phillip was called "the Bold" for his abilities in combat, not his political or personal character. He ruled for 15 years, dying of illness in southern France in the Aragonese Crusade. He was born in Poissy, a favorite place for the French royal family to stay since the 12th century. He is buried in the Basilica of St. Denis.

Edward I, King of England, Plantagenet:
Edward ruled for 35 years during the 13th century. He was born in the Palace of Westminster, London, built in 1016, which is open to the public at various time. He died at Burgh by Sands, a small village in Cumbria, England, on his way to war against the Scots and is buried at Westminster Abbey, London.

Henry III of England, Plantagenet:
Henry was king from age 9 but actually ruled for only 24 of his 56-year reign. He was born in Winchester Castle, Hampshire, founded in 1057. The Great Hall and excavated remains of the round tower are open to the public. Henry died at the Palace of Westminster, London, and is buried at Westminster Abbey.

14th century

Isabella of France, Queen of England:
When Isabella married King Edward II in the 14th century, she brought with her a direct lineage to the kings of France. Although she originally supported her husband, she turned against him, organized an army to

The Conciergerie (left) was part of the Palais de la Cité in Paris. Winchester Castle, Hampshire, was built in 1067 and for over one hundred years was the seat of government of the Norman kings.

depose him and become regent on behalf of her son, Edward III, and may have arranged Edward II's murder. The daughter of King Philip IV of France, Isabella was brought up at the Chateau du Louvre, which was destroyed during the 16th century, and Palais de la Cité in Paris. The facade of the castle can be seen along the banks of the Seine and a portion of the palace, now known as the Conciergerie, is open to the public. Isabelle died in Hertford Castle, England; only the gatehouse remains of the original castle and is open to the public. She was buried at Christ Church Greyfriars on Newgate Street, London, destroyed in the Great Fire of 1666 and again in the Blitz of 1940; a public memorial garden with ruins of the church remains.

John of Gaunt, 1st Duke of Plantagenet:
John owned three castles in England, all of which are now in ruins and open to the public. Bolingbrook Castle was built in 1220 in Bolingbroke, Lincolnshire; Kenilworth Castle, was founded in 1120 in Warwickshire; and Leicester Castle was built in about 1070 in County Leicestershire. John of Gaunt was a patron and close friend of the poet Geoffrey Chaucer, who wrote *Book of the Duchess* in commemoration of John's first wife, Blanche of Lancaster.

Edward III, King of England, Plantagenet:
Edward, who ruled for 50 years, was born in Windsor Castle, London. The castle, which originally was built in the 11th century, with reconstruction continuing to the present, is open to the public. He is buried in Westminster Abby, founded in 960. The present church building, begun in 1245, is open to the public.

Duke John of Gaunt owned Kenilworth Castle (above), founded in 1120 in Warwickshire, England and Leicester Castle, built in about 1070 in County Leicestershire, England.

Mary Gostwick ancestry: The marriage of another Spencer, Nicholas, to Mary Gostwick in the 16th century links our family directly to the English kings before the Norman Conquest and to the Kings of Scotland. Little is known about the residences of these early kings because, before the Normans, most castles were built of earth and timber. Their tombs were moved when the original abbeys where they were buried were rebuilt.

9th century

Alfred "the Great," King of Wessex and the Anglo-Saxons:
Ruling for 28 years, Alfred is known for successfully defending his kingdom against Viking conquest, promoting education and improving the kingdom's legal system, military structure and general quality of life. He was born in the village of Wanating (now Wantage in Oxfordshire); he died in Winchester and is buried at Hyde Abbey, Winchester, Hampshire, which was demolished in 1539.

10th century

Edward "the Elder," King of the Anglo-Saxons:
Edward ruled for 25 years. He died in Farndon, Cheshire, England, after quelling a revolt against Mercians and Welshmen. He was buried in Hyde Abbey in Winchester, Hampshire, with his father, Alfred the Great. A new cathedral was built in Winchester after the Norman Conquest, and the monks of New Minster moved to the nearby Abbey of Hyde.

Edmund "the Magnificent," King of England:
Edmund ruled for seven years. He was born in Wessex, which means "the kingdom of the West Saxons." He was murdered by a thief while attending St. Augustine's Day mass in Pucklechurch in South Gloucestershire. He was buried in Glastonbury Abbey. The abbey was founded in the 7th century and enlarged in the 10th. It was destroyed by fire in

King Edmund of England was buried at Glastonbury Abbey left). Queen Isabella of England was buried at Hertford Castle. Both now are in ruins.

1184, was rebuilt then fell victim to the Dissolution of the Monasteries in 1536. The ruins of the abbey are set in 36 acres of parkland and open to the public.

Edgar "the Peaceful," King of England:
Edgar was king for a relatively peaceful 16 years. He died in Winchester, Hampshire, England, and was buried in Glastonbury Abbey in Glastonbury, Somerset, England.

Aethelred II "the Unready," King of the English:
He reigned for 27 years in the 10th and early 11th centuries, a time that was marked by continuous raids led by Sweyn, King of Denmark, who wanted to rule England. Cnut the Great, Sweyn's son, conquered most of England while Aethelred defended London. Aethelred died in London and was buried in Old St. Paul's Cathedral, London. The tomb and his monument were destroyed along with the cathedral in the Great Fire of London in 1666.

Malcolm I MacAlpin, King of Scotland:
Malcolm ruled for 11 years during the 10th century, becoming king when his cousin Constantine abdicated to become a monk. Malcolm was killed defending the north of his kingdom by men of Moray at Fetteresso, near Aberdeen. He is buried at Saint Orans Chapel Cemetery on the Isle of Iona in the Inner

Bellingham Castle, County Louth, Ireland (above), served as the ancestral home for Bellinghams since the 17th century. Kings of Scotland are buried in Saint Oran's Chapel Cemetery on the Isle of Iona, off the west coast of Scotland.

Hebrides, a center of Gaelic monasticism from the 6th century. Iona is difficult to get to but worth the effort.

Kenneth II, King of Scotland (or Alba in Scottish Gaelic), MacKenneth:
The Scottish kings lived in Glamis, County Angus, a Scottish conservation village with ancient carved Pictish stones. The parish church was founded in the 8th century, but has been rebuilt several times. In Shakespeare's *Macbeth*, MacBeth is the Thane of Glamis. Kenneth II ruled for 24 years in the 10th century. Typical of the times, his rule was marked by treachery and he was killed by his own men in Fettercairn. He may be buried on the Isle of Iona.

Malcolm II, King of Scotland, MacKenneth:
Malcolm II succeeded to the throne after he killed the previous king, his cousin Kenneth III. He ruled for 29 years, demonstrating a rare ability among early Scottish kings to survive in the 11th century. Because he had no sons, he secured the loyalty of rivals by negotiating marriages to them for his daughters. He was buried at Saint Orans Chapel Cemetery on the Isle of Iona.

Rebecca Claiborn ancestry: Robert Coleman's father married Rebecca Claiborne, who lived and died in Suffolk, England. Rebecca may have been the sister of William Claiborne, who arrived in Jamestown, Virginia, in 1621 to work as a surveyor. He became a wealthy planter, trader and a major figure in the politics of the colonies.

The Neville family built Hornby Castle in Lancashire, England, in the 13th century.

William was the forebearer of a number of lines of American Claibornes, including William C. C. Claiborne, first governor of Louisiana, and fashion designer Liz Claiborne.

Through the Claibornes, we are directly related to the Bellinghams, Lancastors, Crackanthorps, Sandfords, Radcliffes, Nevilles, de Traffords, de Venables and many others too numerous to research. Grace Bellingham of Wesmoreland was Robert Coleman's great-grandmother through the Claiborne line. The Bellingham family at different times held three baronetcies, one in England and two in Ireland. The most recent was the village of Castlebellingham in County Louth, Ireland. The castle there, which served as the ancestral home for Bellinghams since the 17th century, now provides bed and breakfast accommodations and is available for weddings and special events.

Howgill Castle in Milburn, England, belonged to the Lancaster family in the 14th and 15th centuries and passed from them to the Crackanthorpe and Sandford families. The castle was built in the last quarter of the 14th century with improvements in the 17th and 18th centuries. Howgill Castle is privately owned and can be seen near Milburn.

Sir William Radcliffe built Ordsall Hall in Salford, Manchester, in the 15th century. The building has been restored and now is open to the public as a period house and local museum. The house was the scene of the 1842 novel *Guy Fawkes*. An episode of the television program *Most Haunted* was filmed there in 2005.

Our Neville ancestors built Hornby Castle in Lancashire in the 13th century. The castle was rebuilt and restored in the 18th and 19th

Sir William Radcliffe built Ordsall Hall (above) in Salford, Manchester, in the 15th century. Howgill Castle in Milburn, England, has belonged to the Lancaster, Crackanthorpe and Sandford families from the 14th century.

centuries. The privately owned property is recorded in the National Heritage List for England as a designated Grade I listed building. The gardens are open to the public for special events and the castle may be seen from a distance.

Trafford Park in Lancashire was the ancestral estate of our ancestor Lady Jane de Trafford, born in 1425. The de Traffords were one of the most ancient families in England, and one of the largest landowners in Stretford, Greater Manchester. The family acquired the lands around Trafford in about 1200 but didn't locate their home to the park until about 1720. Trafford Park contained Trafford Hall, its grounds, and three farms: Park Farm, Moss Farm, and Waters Meeting Farm. The property that had been described as a "beautifully timbered deer park" was redeveloped as an industrial park in the late 19th century.

Sir Edmond Trafford married our ancestor, Alice de Venables, in about 1420. The de Venables, from Venables in Normandy, were followers of William the Conqueror who came to England after the Norman Conquest of 1066. They were Barons of Kinderton in Middlewich, Cheshire, from the 12th through the 18th centuries. The principal landmark in Middlewich is the 12th century Anglican parish church of St. Michael and All Angels, which is open to the public. The remains of Kinderton Hall and its moated site are also located there.

James Crewes
9th great-grandfather, Walker line

James Crewes is best known for being hanged as a participant in Bacon's Rebellion, an armed rebellion in 1676 by Virginia settlers led by Nathaniel Bacon. Within our Walker ancestry, though, his most important contribution may be the small amount of Native DNA he added through his relationship with Moriah Bland. The story is reported in this account by researcher David Douglass:

> *In the folk lore of colonial Virginia comes a story that reads more like a historical romance novel than the pages of a high school history book. James Crewes it is said, took as a consort from among his Native servants, a young Native American woman who has come to be known by the name, Moriah Bland. In some accounts she is said to have been Powhatan, perhaps related to Pocahontas and in other accounts she is a Cherokee mistress, and the daughter of a famous chief. And Hannah Crewes who along with her husband Giles Carter was named in the will of James Crewes is said to have been the illegitimate daughter of James Crewes*

and Moriah. There are no existing records that prove this family tradition and that is not surprising. At that time, relationships between white men and Native women were not uncommon but were looked upon unfavorably and such relationships were made illegal in 1691. Though hard proof is lacking, it is a persistent and often repeated story among the descendants of Giles and Hannah Carter that Hannah was the child of James Crewes and his Native American consort. . . . Like every great story it has foundations in fact. The characters are real historical figures, they lived and died. But just where fact ends and fiction begins has been blurred by the passage of time and an embellished telling and retelling of the story.

James Crewes was the son of Robert Crewes of London, a prosperous merchant in partnership with his two older sons, Edward and Francis. As the youngest son, it makes sense that he would have been sent to Virginia to expand the family business. In Virginia, James became a prosperous planter—probably tobacco—and trader in fur pelts.

James Crewes arrived in Virginia at about the same time as Giles Carter. A number of researchers believe that Giles was James' business partner. Giles was recorded as coming to Virginia as a headright of planter William Fry. In theory, that means that Fry would have received 50 acres of land for paying for Giles' passage to Virginia and Giles would work for him for several years to repay his debt. However, the headright system was often abused, with some planters claiming headright for men born in Virginia. It is possible that Giles Carter may

James Crewes was hanged for his role in the burning of Jamestown, as depicted in a painting by National Park Service artist Sidney E. King.

never have worked for William Fry but came to Virginia with the intent of working with James Crewes.

James wrote his will in 1676, perhaps in anticipation of the trouble that occurred for his participation in Bacon's Rebellion. In the will, he referred to Giles Carter as "my loving friend," with the wish that Giles should live in his house and command his servants. He gave Giles and his wife Hannah the use of the plantation during both of their lives, rent free, "only paying one Graine of Indian Corn when demanded." He also left bequests to Giles' and Hannah's children, Mary, Susan and Theodrick Carter.

Bacon's Rebellion was an armed rebellion in 1676 by Virginia settlers led by Nathaniel Bacon against the rule of Governor William Berkeley. Berkeley's failure to address demands of the colonists regarding their safety from attacks by Natives and his refusal to allow Bacon to be a part of Berkeley's fur trade with the Natives helped to motivate the uprising.

Both Crewes and Bacon had been elected to the General Assembly but Governor Berkeley used his influence over other members to deny them permission to retaliate against attacks by Natives. A thousand Virginians rose up in arms against Berkeley, drove him from Jamestown and burned the capital. Berkeley called for government forces from England to defeat the resistance, the first rebellion in the American colonies in which discontented frontiersmen took part.

Before an English naval squadron could arrive to aid Berkeley and his forces, Bacon became ill and died in October 1676. Governor Berkeley seized the property of rebels for the colony and executed 23 men by hanging including James Crewes. After an investigative committee returned a report to King Charles II criticizing Berkeley's handling of the situation, he was relieved of the governorship and recalled to England.

The name Crewes is a variant spellings of Crew, Cruise, Cruse, Cruwys and Crouse. Originally, it identified someone who was from the town of Crewe, located near the Welsh Marches (borderland) in Cheshire, England. The name may also be of French habitational origin from "Cruys-Straete" in Nord, from the Gaulish word "crodiu," hard.

One Richard de Crues was recorded in the Curia Rolls of Devonshire in 1214, while the Hundred Rolls of Bedfordshire list a Robert Cruse in 1275. Sir Thomas Crew or Crewe was a speaker of the House of Commons in the 17th century. Baron Crew was a title in the Peerage of England created on 1661 for the politician John Crew. The title became extinct on the death of his younger son in 1721.

Elizabeth Gorusch/Gorsuch
8th great-grandmother, Watson line

You probably have heard of Justice Neil Gorsuch, who was appointed to the United States Supreme Court in 2017. There's a good chance he is a relative.

According to sketchy early Virginia records, Elizabeth Gorusch (or Maysel Elizabeth Gorsuch), married William Powell in Isle of Wight County, Virginia, in about 1631. William was a great-grandson of Capt. William Powell, one of the earliest arrivals to the Jamestown, Virginia, settlement in 1609 and lieutenant governor of the colony in 1617.

As Elizabeth Gorusch's husband was a member of a prominent Virginia family, so it would seem likely that Elizabeth also was from a prominent family. My research has discovered no one with the name "Gorusch." However, there are many members of the wealthy Gorsuch family in England, some who settled in Virginia in the 1650s.

Like many other researchers, I have concluded that Elizabeth Gorusch, born in 1618, was somehow related to a Rev. John Gorsuch, born in London, England, in 1600. If John Gorsuch was her father, her mother wasn't Ann Lovelace, whose 1628 marriage to John Gorsuch is recorded in the history books. That means that Elizabeth might have been the child of a previous marriage, or a sister, cousin, or some other relation.

Whatever their relationship, the Gorsuches were an interesting family. Daniel Gorsuch, born in 1569, was a wealthy silk merchant who could afford the best education for his son, John. John Gorsuch received bachelor's, master's and doctor's degrees from Cambridge. Deciding he didn't want to enter the family business, John entered the ministry of the Church of England.

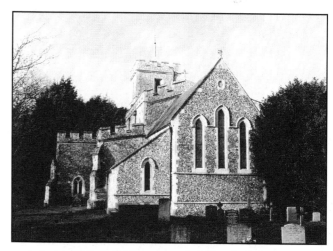

In the late 1620s, Daniel Gorsuch bought St. Mary the Virgin Church in the Hertfordshire town of Walkern and made his son John church rector.

During his youth, John Gorsuch was a close friend of Richard Lovelace. Richard was the son of Sir William Lovelace, a member of the original Virginia Company. Through Richard, John met his wife, Ann Lovelace.

The Gorsuches and Lovelaces were ardent supporters of King Charles, who ruled England, Scotland, and Ireland from 1625 until he was beheaded in 1649. From 1642 until his death, King Charles was at war with his Parliament. In this war, the great majority of the nobles and the gentry, with their dependents, took the side of the king. The middle classes—the traders and manufacturers of the towns, and most of the small farmers—upheld the cause of Parliament. The king's supporters, known as "Cavaliers," believed in the Church of England and enjoyed the finer things of life. The supporters of Parliament were mainly sober-minded Puritans, plain in their lives and in their dress.

John Gorsuch obtained his church posting in a way we might find surprising today. During the 1600s, private landholders often built and maintained local Anglican churches, particularly in the rural areas of England. The parish churches would be in the care of a rector or priest who collected the church tithes (really local property taxes). The rector used them to support himself and the operations of the church, and sometimes to pay a return to the private investor.

In the late 1620s, Daniel Gorsuch began investing in real estate in Hertfordshire, located between London and Cambridge. One of the properties he bought was St. Mary the Virgin Church in the Hertfordshire town of Walkern. Daniel Gorsuch spent no small amount of money refurbishing the church. So it probably was no coincidence that the new Rev. John Gorsuch became rector of St. Mary in 1632. St. Mary still stands today. It is the oldest village church in Hertfordshire, with a Saxon wall and rare chalk rood (crucifix) dating back to the mid-10th century.

This brick farmhouse replaced the original Gorsuch Hall which was destroyed by fire in 1816.

Rev. Gorsuch, being a strong supporter of the King and the traditional rules of the Church of England, refused to allow Puritan practices in his church. When the parishioners complained to an Anglican bishop with Puritan leanings, Rev. Gorsuch was overruled. The bishop was arrested by King Charles and imprisoned.

As the English Civil War began in 1642, a pro-Puritan vicar named Simon Smeath lodged charges of public drunkenness, gambling, malfeasance and insubordination against Rev. Gorsuch. Smeath had powerful friends in Parliament who removed Gorsuch from the church his father owned and installed Smeath as his replacement. What Smeath didn't understand was that, because the Gorsuch family still owned the church, they were entitled to a share of the tithes. In 1647, Smeath complained to authorities that Rev. Gorsuch was "causing a nuisance" in the community by trying to collect his family's share of the tithes. When the men went to Gorsuch's home, he tried to hide in the hayloft, where they found him and smothered him to death.

Ann Lovelace Gorsuch was now a widow with many children, no stable means of support, and a questionable reputation with the Puritan authorities. Her political problem wasn't just the suspicious death of her Royalist husband but also the Royalist activities of her famous Lovelace brothers. Richard Lovelace was a prolific writer who is remembered as the poet who wrote "Stone walls do not a prison make/Nor iron bars a cage," while he was imprisoned for supporting the king during the English Civil War.

Richard's brother, Francis Lovelace, fought in Royalist units in England and Wales, rising to the rank of colonel. In 1650, when Francis obtained permission to immigrate to America, his widowed sister Ann Gorsuch and several of her children accompanied him.

Gorsuch is not a common surname. Only about 3,400 Gosuches were recorded worldwide in 2014. More than 3,000 of those were living in the United States and probably descend from the early Gorsuch immigrants to Virginia.

The Gorsuch name originated in the small village of Scarisbrick, Lancashire, England, site of the ruins of Scarisbrick Hall, built in the 13th century. Scarisbrick was the home of Walter de Scarisbrick who had two sons, Henry, his heir and Adam. As the Scarisbrick estate would pass to Henry, Walter assigned land to Adam at a place called Gosfordsyke (the place where the geese ford the creek). Adam took as his surname the place name de Gosfordsyke, later shortened to Gorsuch. The name Gorsuch was applied to an estate there in the 1600's and a Gorsuch Lane remains there today. A brick farmhouse, named Gorsuch Hall, replaced an earlier hall destroyed by fire in 1816.

Capt. Henry Isham
10th great-grandfather, Walker line

Capt. Henry Isham was a successful merchant and landowner in early Virginia, but he is best known for his daughter Mary's marriage to Col. William Randolph. Mary Isham was born about 1658 in Bermuda Hundred. In 1678, she married Col. Randolph, who had immigrated in 1674 and settled on Turkey Island in Henrico County, Virginia. William Randolph was a member of the House of Burgesses and served as its speaker in 1698.

Mary Randolph bore nine children, seven sons and two daughters. Her daughter, Jane, was the wife of Peter Jefferson and mother to Thomas Jefferson, the third president of the United States. Son Richard and daughter Anne married members of the Bolling family who were descendants of Thomas Rolfe, the only child of Pocahontas. Her daughter Mary's son William Stith was the third president of William and Mary College. His grandfather William Randolph had helped found the college and also served as a trustee.

Henry Isham was born in about 1627 in Pytchley, Northamptonshire, England, a second son to parents William and Mary Brett Isham. In 1656, he immigrated to Bermuda Hundred, Henrico, Virginia, situated along the James River, He married Katherine Banks, daughter of Christopher Banks, and they had nine children.

Henry Isham's father, William Isham and his wife, Mary Brett, lived in Pytchley, Northamptonshire. William's wife outlived him by more than

Lamport Hall in Lamport, Northamptonshire, was the home of the Isham family from 1560 to 1976.

50 years but probably remained in England. William Isham's father was Sir Euseby Isham, who was knighted in 1603.

The surname Isham was first found in Northamptonshire at Isham, a Saxon village and civil parish that dates back to 974 when it was listed as Ysham. In *The Domesday Book* of 1086, the place name was listed with the present spelling of Isham. The place name literally means "homestead by the River Ise," having derived from the Celtic river name plus the Old English "ham" for home. Northhamptonshire must have suited the Isham family well because they never wandered far from it until Henry Isham went to the Virginia colony.

Lamport Hall in Lamport, Northamptonshire, was the home of the Isham family from 1560 to 1976. Like the Colemans, the Ishams were wealthy wool merchants during the 16th and 17th centuries. In 1568 John Isham built a manor house on the Lamport Estate. His grandson, also named John, became the first baronet in 1627 during the reign of Charles I, and Sir Justinian Isham built the main existing building in 1655. Tenth baronet Sir Charles Isham is credited with beginning the tradition of garden gnomes in the United Kingdom when he introduced a number of terracotta figures from Germany in the 1840s.

By about 1950 the house had considerably deteriorated, and the then owner Sir Gyles Isham undertook major renovation works and allowed the ground floor to be opened to the public in 1974. When he died he left the building and its contents to the Lamport Hall Preservation Trust, who care for the Hall and Gardens today. The Isham family lived at Lamport Hall for over 400 years.

William Leake
7th great-grandfather, Watson line

Who doesn't love a good "evil stepmother" story? This one involves our immigrant ancestor, William Leake.

Hon. Shelton F. Leake in Charlottsville, Virginia, told the story to his nephew in a letter. He related how William Leake's father, Walter Leake, was a very wealthy landowner on the borderland between England and Wales. William's mother died when he was an infant and his father married a second wife by whom he had several children.

According to England's laws at that time, William, as the eldest son, would have inherited his father's estate. However, while the father was away, the stepmother had William kidnapped and sent to Virginia. As it happened, a band of gypsies was in the area at the time, so the stepmother persuaded her husband that they had stolen his son. Although the father offered huge rewards for his son's return, William could not be found. The story supposedly was later confirmed by a descendant of the stepmother's children who then lived in New England.

We don't know when William Leake arrived in Virginia, but if the story is true, he may have been very young. It is believed that he came to Virginia from Nottinghamshire, the home of the heroic outlaw Robin Hood, as did his wife, Mary Bostick. Mary arrived in Virginia with her father, William Bostick, in 1684 when she was 14 years old. That's the same year she married William.

William and Mary Leake had at least five children, all born in St. Peter's Parish and listed in the parish register. Their home in Goochland named Rocky Spring remained continuously in the family for many generations. There is a small town called East Leake in Goochland County, where the family cemetery is located, that likely was the site of the family home.

The descendants of William and Mary Leake have a distinguished history in Virginia and other states. They include many lawyers, legislators, judges and military leaders. Among them was Hon. Walter Leake, who was a Revolutionary War soldier and a member of the Virginia legislature. Leake was appointed judge of Mississippi Territory by Thomas Jefferson, served as Mississippi's first U. S. senator and was the third governor of Mississippi.

Sutton Scarsdale Hall, just outside of Chesterfield, Derbyshire, was owned by the Leke/Leake family for nearly 350 years.

The surname Leake is probably of Norman origin. A Luke de Lec is mentioned in church records in France in 1208. There are towns called Leake in Lincolnshire, Yorkshire and Nottinghamshire. The first listings of the family name in England were John de Lek, Roger de Leke and Theobald de Lek, all on tax rolls in Lincolnshire in 1273.

Sutton Scarsdale Hall, just outside of Chesterfield, Derbyshire, was owned by the Leke/Leake family for nearly 350 years. The original Saxon estate, built in the 10th century, was purchased by John Leke of Nottinghamshire in the 15th century. It was modernized by Francis Leke, the 1st Earl of Scarsdale. In the 17th century, Nicholas Leke, the 4th and last Earl of Scarsdale, commissioned the building of a Georgian mansion using parts of the existing structure. After years of neglect, the estate was gutted and stripped in 1920. Scarsdale Hall now is an elaborate ruin that is in the care of English Heritage and is freely accessible to visitors.

Thomas Mask
8th great-grandfather, Watson line

The Mask family became entwined with our Coleman-Watson ancestors in early Virginia through the 1710 marriage of Judith Mask and Walter Leake. Judith's father was immigrant Thomas Mask's son, John Mask, and William was the son of immigrant William Leake.

Judith Mask's mother was Martha Ann Christian, daughter of immigrant Thomas Christian. The marriage between Judith Mask and Walter Leake produced Elizabeth Leake, who, in 1751, married James Coleman, great-grandson of immigrant Robert Coleman. The daughter of Elizabeth and James, Lucinda Lucy Coleman, married Evan Thomas Watson.

What little is known about the Mask family in Virginia is summarized in an account by Dalia Matos Mask on her family history website:

> *The earliest Mask men to arrive in the Virginia Colony were: Thomas Mask (who arrived in 1638), William Mask (1652) and Thomas Mask (1653). They came mostly as indentured servants, that is they promised to work seven years for someone to secure payment for their passage over. Some of them obtained land of their own and became tobacco planters. The family is mentioned frequently in New Kent County, Virginia, in the records of St. Peter's Parish and subsequently in St. Paul's Parish. When St. Peter's Parish was divided in 1704, the Mask*

family lived within the boundaries of the newly formed St. Paul's Parish. A John Mask was one of the original five trustees for the new parish.

That they were in early Virginia is confirmed in records beginning in 1690 of "processioning," a method of confirming property lines by having all the property owners within a small area walk the property lines together every four years. The Masks were in each processioning from 1690 until 1767, first in St. Peter's and then in St. Paul's Parish. In the 1767 processioning, John Mask, William Mask and "Thomas Mask's heirs" were shown. The 1771 processioning showed "William Mask, deceased." The Mask name doesn't appear after that date. Later records were destroyed by fire during the Civil War.

Because the Masks arrived in Virginia as indentured servants probably indicates that they were not descendants of landed gentry. That being the case, there are few records outside of the occasional church record regarding their family history in England.

The surname Mask is relatively rare. There were less than 7,000 Masks worldwide in 2014, with more than half of those in the United States. Surprisingly, the second and third highest incidences of the name are in Egypt and Morocco.

Sources vary widely regarding the origins of the surname Mask, ranging from Comaskey or Comiskey in Northern Ireland; Marshall, Marescal or Maskall in England and Germany; Maskew or Mascau in France; and Malatestas in Italy.

I think the *Surname DB* website offers the most reasonable explanation for the origin of the Mask name:

> *Last name: Maskew This interesting and rare name is of French origin and is the Anglicization of the French surname Mascau, thought to have some association with the French word 'masque,' meaning a mask. Maskew, Mascoe or Mascau, was introduced into England in the mid-16th century with the large numbers of Huguenot exiles, escaping religious persecution in France, who settled in Britain, during the 16th and 17th centuries. The Coat of Arms for Mascau is listed in Rietstap's General Armory, as a blue shield with a severed hand clad in chain mail holding an upright sword. Amongst the sample recordings in London are the christenings of Jeanne Mascau on December 13th 1629, and Marie Mascau on January 12th 1634, both at the French Huguenot Church, Threadneedle Street, and Mary Maskew in December 1613 at St. Dunstan's, Stepney. The first recorded spelling of the family name*

is shown to be that of Sendeloo Maskoo, which was dated June 12th 1562, St. Botolph's, Bishopsgate, London, during the reign of Queen Elizabeth 1.

Helen Metland/Maitland
6th great-grandmother, Watson line

Helen Metland was a member of the powerful Scottish Clan Maitland. Her Maitland ancestors were barons and earls who owned Thirlestane Castle, Tibbers Castle and Lennoxlove House. They led battles and lost their lives in military campaigns fought between Scotland and England in the 13th and 14th centuries. For their loyalty and service to the crown, they were rewarded with the Earldom of Lauderdale, a title that continues to this day.

Helen was born in 1682 in Kirkcaldy, Fife, a town near Edinburgh on the east coast of Scotland. Her father, George Maitland, was a merchant in Aberdeen. She married William Black in about 1717 and had 11 or 12 children before the family immigrated to Virginia in about 1735. Eight sons accompanied them and settled in the colonies. Whether any of the daughters immigrated is not known.

Helen died at the birth of her last son, James, in 1740 in Onslow, North Carolina. William sold his property then, "reserving 12 square feet for burial ground in the field," according to Onslow County Deed Book C, 40. William moved to Chesterfield County, Virginia, after Helen's death.

The lands of Lethington (now Lennoxlove House) were owned by the Maitland family from 1345 to 1682.

The Maitland Clan descends from a Norman companion of William the Conqueror who joined him in conquering England in 1066 and later settled in Northumberland. The name originally was Mautalent.

The Mautalents come from the village of Les Moitiers d'Allonne near Carteret in Normandy. The first time the name is found in Scotland was Thomas de Matulant of Lauderdale in the 12th century. During the reign of King Alexander III of Scotland, Thomas's grandson, Sir Richard Matulant was one of the most powerful Lowland barons, owning the lands of Thirlestane, Blythe, Tollus and Hedderwick. He supported Robert de Brus at the Battle of Bannockburn in 1314.

Two Maitlands were named Lords of Thirlestane in the 15th and 16th centuries, and 18 were Earls of Lauderdale from the 17th century to present day. In the 17th century, John Maitland was named both Earl and Duke of Lauderdale, Earl of Guilford and Baron Petersham. Because he left no male heir, his dukedom became extinct, but he was succeeded in the earldom by his brother.

Thirlestane Castle, which served as the seat of the Earls of Lauderdale, is set in extensive parklands near Lauder in the Scottish Borders area near Edinburgh. The land has been in the ownership of the Maitland family since 1587. The castle was substantially extended in the 1670s by John Maitland, the Duke of Lauderdale. Further additions to Thirlestane Castle were made in the 19th century. The castle is now cared for by a charitable trust, and is open to the public.

The lands of Lethington were acquired in 1345 by Robert Maitland of Thirlestane. The Maitland family constructed the earliest part of

The Maitland family has owned Thirlestane Castle in Lauder, Scotland, since 1587.

the Lethington castle, the L-plan tower house at the southwest of the building, which was burned by English troops in 1549. Lethington, near Haddington, remained in the Maitland family until after the death of John Maitland, Duke of Lauderdale in 1682. The Lethington Castle, now known as Lennoxlove House, is home to one of Scotland's most important collections of portraits, including works by Anthony van Dyck, Canaletto, Sir Peter Lely, Sir Godfrey Kneller, Sir Henry Raeburn, and others. It also houses important pieces of furniture, porcelain and other fine artifacts.

Tibbers Castle lands were granted to John Mautaland of Thirlestane by the Earl of March in 1369 when Mautaland married the earl's sister Agnes. His son, Sir Robert Mautaland, obtained a crown charter of the land. Tibbers Castle was a motte-and-bailey castle overlooking a ford across the River Nith in Dumfries and Galloway, Scotland. While it is unclear at what point Tibbers Castle fell out of use, by the 18th century the site was used for agriculture. Several archaeological investigations have taken place there since 1864.

Richard New
9th great-grandfather, Watson line; 8th great-grandfather, Walker line

The marriage of two daughters of Virginia planter Edmund New and a will witnessed by their husbands in the early 1700s indelibly links the histories of both our Watson and Walker families.

In the tradition of his English forbearers, Edmund New arranged marriages for some of his 12 children that helped to maintain and enhance his wealth and influence. It was through two such marriages that our family lines crossed and maintained close ties from the earliest days of the nation's history.

We know this because in 1726 Edmund New rewrote his will. The second version, filed with the Henrico County Court a year after his death, was only slightly different from the first written a year earlier. However, one aspect of it has profound implications for the history of both the Watson and Walker families: the witnesses were Watson ancestor Thomas Christian and Walker ancestor John Tully.

Thomas Christian married Edmund New's eldest daughter, Rebecca, in 1680. John Tully married New's ninth child, Sarah, in 1710. The document verifies that Watson and Walker family ancestors were related and closely linked nearly 300 years ago.

Edmund New's father was the immigrant Richard New from Bristol, England, who was just 16 or 17 years old when he signed on to work for Virginia plantation owners Edward Travis and John Johnson. Although we don't know the ship he sailed aboard to cross the Atlantic, he was listed as being one of several persons transported in 1637 by Travis and Johnson, planters who received 900 acres in James City County that same year.

This record suggests that Richard New came to the New World as an indentured servant. These young men and women, most under the age of 21, typically contracted to work for between three and seven years in exchange for transportation, food, clothing, lodging and other necessities during the term of indenture. Most became helpers on farms or house servants. In terms of living conditions and discipline, they were usually treated like relatives. They were not paid cash. It was a system that provided jobs and, most important, transportation for poor young people from the overcrowded labor markets of Europe who wanted to come to labor-short America but had no money to pay for it.

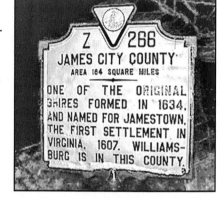

Although Richard New arrived a poor man to Virginia, by 1655 he had managed to raise his status to landowner thanks to a generous gift from Capt. Francis Barrett. The records are unclear as to why Capt. Barrett granted property to Richard New, but the Virginia Legislature, in July 1653, includes Richard New as one of several individuals who had been granted special license to receive "charitable benevolence of well disposed persons."

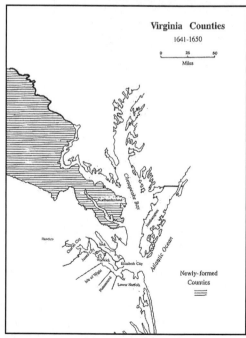

> *Upon the humble petition of John Claxsonn an old Virginian, and the testimony of the commissioners of the countie of Yorke where he lived of the great loss he sustained by fire to his utter undoeing, not abot to maintain himselfe and five children, The Grand Assembly duely weighing his distressed estate hath granted him the said Claxsonn, an order as a breife to gather the charitable benevolence of well disposed persons. The like also is granted unto Thomas Bagwell of the Isle of Wight county and to **Richard New of James Cittie county.***

In 1655, Richard New was assigned 750 acres in James City County, Virginia, on the north side of the James River and east side of Chickahomania River, across the James River from Edward Travis. The land patent states that Richard's land adjoined land of Thomas Brookes and Mr. Rolph. This Mr. Rolph would be Thomas Rolphe, son of John Rolphe and Pocahontas, daughter of Chief Powhatan. The patent also states that this land was "for the transport of 15 persons—15 Irishmen included in a certificate granted unto Capt. Barrett, March last, and assigned unto said New."

Most researchers agree that the reason Capt. Barrett assigned a grant of property to Richard New probably was because Richard married Barrett's daughter, Agnes. Records confirming Richard New's marriage have not been found but it is known that he had at least seven children, and also may have been married to Mary Huflett.

Some details of Richard New's origins in England were recorded in "The Family of New" by Ann Wall Allgood and Janet New Huff:

> *No ship record has been found concerning Richard New, but it is the opinion of Dr. John E. Manahan of Charlottesville, Virginia, a descendant of Richard New, that the family was from Gloucestershire County (probably Bristol), England. Research of the English records shows that the family of New or Newe were living in Bristol in 1491. The will of Edmund Newe of Bristol, dated 16 Jan 1491, has been preserved; it states that he was Burgess of the Town of Bristol, and Dyer, and that he was buried in the Church of St. Thomas. His wife was Agnes and his children were John, Richard, Robert, and Margaret. We feel reasonably sure that this Edmund Newe was an ancestor of Richard New, the immigrant. The family of New in Bristol in the 1700s were shipwrights.*

The surname New was first found in Cambridgeshire, England, where Richard le Newe was listed in tax rolls of 1273. The same rolls also listed Robert le New in Wiltshire and Simon le Neue in Bedfordshire.

Colonel William Randolph
8th great-grandfather, Walker line

William Randolph came from humble beginnings to become one of the most influential American colonists, landowners, planters, merchants and politicians.

William was about 20 years old when he arrived in Virginia between 1669-1672. Although he had little capital and few connections in England or Virginia, he was able to begin acquiring property fairly quickly. He may have started by building houses but by 1674, he had acquired enough money to import 12 persons into the colony, earning land patents for 600 acres of land. By 1697, he had imported 72 servants and 690 slaves and collected patents for more than 7000 acres.

William was born in Moreton Morrell, Warwickshire, England, in 1651, the second of seven children of Richard Randolph and Elizabeth Rylan. His grandfather, Richard Randolph, was a steward and servant to Baron Edward la Zouche. His father probably served in a similar capacity, but his residences are not recorded.

William's uncle, the poet Thomas Randolph, attended Westminster School and Cambridge University on scholarship, but there is no record of other members of the Randolph family attending public school or university. In the 1600s, the family moved to Dublin, where both parents died before 1672.

Another of William's uncles, Henry Randolph, immigrated to Virginia around 1642 and probably encouraged William to join him there. The first record of William's residence in the colony was in 1672, when he witnessed a land transaction.

Dungeness and Tuckahoe were Virginia plantations owned by William Randolph's sons.

In about 1675, William married Mary Isham, whose father Henry Isham was a plantation owner from a gentry family who had married a wealthy widow, Katherina Banks Royall. Mary Isham's brother died in 1678, making her the heiress of her father's large estate, Bermuda Hundred, on the James River in Henrico County. William also acquired the property of Nathaniel Bacon, which was forfeited when Bacon was hanged for organizing Bacon's Rebellion against the colonial government. By his death in 1711, it is estimated that William Randolph owned more than 20,000 acres of land in Surry and Henrico counties.

William Randolph built a mansion on the Turkey Island plantation on high ground overlooking the island and the river. It featured a ribbed dome and was known as the "Bird's Cage." He and Mary raised their children there, nine of whom lived to adulthood. His sons added to the family holdings Tuckahoe plantation, Curles plantation, Dungeness plantation and Tazewell plantation. One served as governor of Virginia, another was knighted and was a speaker of the Virginia House of Burgesses. Most married into other prominent Virginia families, including the Blands, Byrds, Carters, Beverleys, Fitzhughs, and Harrisons.

The Randolphs and their descendants continued to dominate politics in Virginia for generations. Edmund Randolph was an aid-de-camp to George Washington in the American Revolutionary War. He was afterward seventh governor of Virginia, the second secretary of state, and the first United States attorney general.

Robert Fitz Randolph, third Lord of Middleham and Spennithorne, built Middleham Castle (above) in Wensleydale and the Church of St. Michael and All the Angels in Spennithorne in the 12th century.

Thomas Jefferson was a great-grandson of William Randolph. Not only was Jefferson the principal author of the Declaration of Independence, he served as a wartime governor of Virginia, an ambassador to France, the first United States secretary of state under President George Washington, the second vice president under John Adams, and third president of the United States. As president, he oversaw the Louisiana Purchase which doubled the size of the United States, and later founded the University of Virginia.

John Marshall, great-grandson of Thomas Randolph of Tuckahoe, was the fourth chief justice of the United States. Previously, he had served as a representative to the U.S. Congress and was secretary of state under President John Adams.

"Light Horse Harry" Lee, great-grandson of William Randolph was the ninth governor of Virginia, a Virginia representative to the U.S. Congress and served as an officer in the Continental Army in the American Revolution.

Thomas Mann Randolph Jr., second great-grandson of William Randolph, was a member of both houses of the Virginia General Assembly, a representative in the U.S. Congress, and the 21st governor of Virginia. James Pleasants Jr., great-grandson of William Randolph, was the 22nd governor of Virginia.

Alnwick Castle in Northumberland, England, as painted by Italian artist Canaletto in about 1750, was owned by the Percy family from the 14th century. Below are ruins of the castle, which was founded by the de Vesci family in the 11th century.

Robert E. Lee, second great-grandson of William Randolph, commanded the Confederate Army in the American Civil War and later served as president of Washington College (later Washington and Lee University). George W. Randolph, third great-grandson of William Randolph, was a Confederate States secretary of war.

While William Randolph arrived in Virginia with little more than an invitation from his uncle, the Randolph name in the British Isles has a long and notable history. The surname Randolph was first found in Middleham, Yorkshire, where in 1190, "a splendid castle was built by Robert Fitz-Ranulph."

The Randolph name was well known in Scotland as early as the days of King Robert de Brus. Thomas Randolph, Lord of Stratnith, married the king's sister, Lady Isabel Bruce. His son, Sir Thomas Randolph, was first Earl of Moray. Randolph earldoms continued through several generations until Agnes Randolph married the Earl of Dunbar, who took the title away from the Randolph family.

William Randolph's ancestry has been traced to the Fitz Randolphs of Yorkshire, Lords of Spennithorne. The parish of Spennithorne in lower Wensleydale in North Yorkshire was held by the Saxon Ghilpatric until in the 13th century it was given to Ranulph, a younger son of Ribald, who founded the family of Fitz Randall of Spennithorne. The Fitz Randall family held the manor house as Lords of Spennithorne until about 1518, when

Ruins of Warkworth Castle, Northumberland (above), and Scarborough Castle, North Yorkshire. Both castles were built in the 12th century and taken over by the Percys in the 14th century.

Ralph Fitz Randall died, his son John died shortly after him, and the estate was divided among John's five sisters.

Middleham Castle in Wensleydale was built by Robert Fitz Randolph, third Lord of Middleham and Spennithorne, commencing in 1190. The castle is a compact, massive structure, and though now in ruins, most of the walls are intact. Once the childhood home of Richard III, the castle is open to the public. The Church of St. Michael and All the Angels, which also is said to have been erected by Robert Fitz Randolph, also still stands in Spennithorne.

Through the Randolphs, our family has direct links to the Conyers, de Percys, de Cliffords, de Vescis, de Veres, de Atons, FitzAlans, and many other members of the English nobility with roots in Normandy. Each of these families owned at least one, often more castles.

John Fitz Randolph married Joan Conyers. The Conyers family owned Hornby Castle in Yorkshire during the 15th and 16th centuries. Her father, Christopher Conyers, who was prominent in local politics in northern England, is believed to have had 25 children by two wives. Most of the estate where Joan was born was demolished in 1930. What remains today is a private residence that is not open to the public.

The Randolphs descend from the de Percy family through the Conyers. The de Percys owned Alnwick Castle, Northumberland. The castle was built by Yves de Vesci in the 11th century and purchased by the Percy family in the 14th century. It was featured as Hogwarts in the first two Harry Potter films and has appeared in many other films. It is presently owned by Ralph Percy, 12th Duke of Northumberland, and is open to the public.

In 1322, Sir Henry Percy, my 21st great-grandfather, was made governor of Pickering Castle and of the town and castle of Scarborough, both in North Yorkshire, and was later knighted at

Skipton Castle in Yorkshire, built in the 11th century, was owned by the Clifford family until the 17th century.

York. He was appointed to Edward III's Council in 1327 and was given the Northumberland castle and barony of Warkworth. Pickering Castle was built by the Normans after 1066. The ruins of Pickering Castle still stand and are open to the public.

Scarborough Castle was built on the site of an ancient Bronze Age fort. Anglo-Saxons built a chapel there which was destroyed in 1066. A castle was first built on the site in the 12th century. Henry de Percy occupied the castle from 1308. Today it is a designated ancient monument managed by English Heritage that is open to the public. The castle grounds are reputed to be haunted by three ghosts, among them a Roman soldier.

Warkworth Castle may have been built by Prince Henry of Scotland or King Henry II of England in the 12th century. Henry de Percy took it over in 1328 and the family has continued to make improvements. Elizabeth Seymour inherited the property from her father in 1750. Her husband, Hugh Smithson, changed his name to Hugh Percy, and the castle then descended through the Dukes of Northumberland, a dynasty he founded. It has been in the care of English Heritage since 1984 as a designated ancient monument and English listed building. The castle and grounds are open to the public.

When Henry de Percy, the third Baron Percy, married Lady Idonea de Clifford, daughter of Sir Robert de Clifford, he was named baron of

The de Veres built Heddington Castle (above) at Hedingham in the 11th and 12th centuries and continued to occupy the castle until the 18th century. The Clifford family acquired Appleby Castle (right) in the 13th century.

Clifford in Herefordshire, feudal baron of Skipton in Yorkshire and feudal baron of Appleby in Westmorland. Skipton Castle, a Norman castle built in 1090, was held by the Clifford family until 1676. Today this well-preserved medieval castle is a tourist attraction and private residence.

Clifford Castle also was built during the Norman period. It is now in ruins in the village of Clifford, Herefordshire. The castle currently is on the English Heritage At Risk Register, with the present owners working closely with English Heritage to implement a program to stabilize the structure and prevent further decay.

Appleby-in-Westmorland is a town in Cumbria, in the historic county of Westmorland. Appleby Castle came into possession of Roger de Clifford through marriage in 1264. His son, Robert, inherited the castle in 1282. Appleby Castle now is a private residence that offers guest rooms in the castle, private cottages on the grounds, as well as wedding and conference facilities. Parts of the castle are open to the public for small private tours.

The de Vesci family, an old Norman family originating in Vassy, Calvados, Normandy, built Alnwwick Castle and owned the ruined Kildare Castle in County Kildare, Ireland. Margerie de Vesci, my 21st great-grandmother, married Gilbert de Aton, first Baron of Aton. The de Vesci family held lands in England and Ireland and William de Vesci was among the competitors for the Crown of Scotland.

Arundel Castle was built in the 11th century and is still home of the FitzAlan-Howard family, who are Dukes of Norfolk and Earls of Arundel.

The remains of the tower are the only above-ground remains of Kildare Castle in County Kildare. From the 12th to 15th centuries, the de Vesci family owned Malton Castle on the site in Malton, North Yorkshire, that is now Castle Garden. The castle was demolished and rebuilt several times before the 17th century.

Isabel de Vere, who married William de Aton, also came from an aristocratic family with origins in Normandy. The family's Norman founder in England, Aubrey (Albericus) de Vere, appears in *The Domesday Book* of 1086 as the holder of a large fief in Essex, Cambridgeshire, Huntingdonshire, and Suffolk. He built his castle at Hedingham in the 11th and 12th centuries.

Today, Hedingham Castle, in the village of Castle Hedingham, is the best preserved Norman tower or keep in England. The family also founded the Essex religious houses of Colne Priory, Hatfield Broad Oak Priory and Castle Hedingham Priory. Twenty generations of de Veres headed the family as Earl of Oxford from the 12th to 18th centuries. Hedington Castle is now available for special events.

Eleanor FitzAlan married Henry de Percy, the first Baron Percy. The FitzAlans held the earldom of Arundel from the 13th century as well as the title of Duke of Norfolk, the premier peerage of England, since the 17th century. From the 11th century, Arundel Castle has served as a home and has been in the ownership of the Duke of Norfolk for over 400 years. The castle has been restored and modernized a number of times and today remains the principal seat of the Dukes of Norfolk. Most of the castle and grounds are open to the public.

Joseph and John "Rocky Creek" Watson
5th and 4th great-grandfathers, Watson line

My favorite thing among all that I've learned researching our family links to the Scottish Watson Clan is their motto, "Insperata floruit" which means "It flourished beyond expectation." It's such a modest, self-deprecating motto. "No one expected much of us, but look how we have thrived!"

Like Dr. John Watson's character in Sherlock Holmes novels, most of us are astute but never quite a match for the genius of a Holmes. There are a few Watson geniuses—most notably, Watson, the IBM computer—but like Dr. Watson, most of us are satisfied to use our abilities to serve others in supporting roles:

> *Holmes was a man of habits . . . and I had become one of them . . . a comrade... upon whose nerve he could place some reliance . . . a whetstone for his mind. I stimulated him . . . If I irritated him by a certain methodical slowness in my mentality, that irritation served only to make his own flame-like intuitions and impressions flash up the more vividly and swiftly. Such was my humble role in our alliance.*
> —*from* The Adventure of the Creeping Man

As near as I can determine, our immigrant ancestors are Joseph and John Watson, who arrived in Virginia or Maryland in the mid 1700s. Other researchers should be aware that the information about Joseph and John Watson as immigrants is my theory and a work in progress.

A list of early Virginia settlers includes 26 Watsons who arrived between 1636 and 1653. We actually have two Watson lines in our Watson family tree and it's possible that the James Randall Watson line might descend from those early arrivals. James married Nancy Margaret Watson, the great-granddaughter of John Watson. They married in Texas but no one is sure where James R. came from. Our best evidence to date is that his grandfather may have been Thomas Watson, who settled in

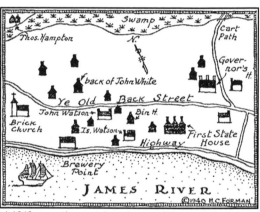

A 1940 excavation map shows homes of Watsons in Jamestown.

The Watson family has leased, then owned Rockingham Castle in Corby, England, since the late 15th century.

Maryland. Some suggest our Virginia line may have been a part of this family who left Maryland to settle in Virginia.

Nancy M. Watson's grandfather was Evan Thomas Watson, a Revolutionary War hero who left Virginia after the war to claim land in the new territories of Kentucky and Texas. His Texas descendants have done considerable research on Evan's line. Most agree that Evan's father was Virginia planter John "Rocky Creek" Watson, so identified to distinguish him from his son John "High Top" Watson. John I purchased land in the northwestern part of Albemarle County on Rocky Creek, and his son, John II, owned property in an area called High Top.

What has been more difficult to determine is who was the immigrant for this line. John Watson could have been a descendant of one of those Watsons who arrived between 1636 and 1653. However, I believe he was the son of Joseph Watson who was listed on a passenger and immigration list for arrival year 1742. Joseph Watson and Mary Gibson were married in Middleton-in-Teesdale, Durham, England, in 1728. They had at least seven children there, among them a John Watson who was baptized in Middleton in 1740.

John was only two years old when Joseph immigrated in 1742, so it is possible his mother and the children may have remained in England and joined Joseph later. There is no information to indicate what Joseph Watson's life in England might have been like. Middleton is near Barnard Castle in Teesdale, but the castle was in ruins at least 100 years before Joseph was born.

The London Lead Company began mining operations in Middleton in 1753, after Joseph left for America. It's possible there were mining operations there before 1753 that went out of business, leaving miners without income to support their families. Another possibility is that Joseph Watson was a tradesman, merchant or a farmer who sold his business or land to parlay his investment into larger holdings in Virginia, but there are no records to confirm either of these theories. Many early Virginia records were destroyed during the Civil War, adding to the difficulty of tracing ancestors who were not among the Virginia elite.

While there is nothing in our history to suggest that our Watson lines are connected to this one, there is a Watson family dynasty in England, complete with a castle to confirm their prosperity. Rockingham Castle is a former royal castle and hunting lodge in Rockingham Forest, a mile to the north from the town center of Corby, Northamptonshire. The Watson family has leased, then owned the castle since the late 15th century. The castle has been the family seat for several Lewis, Edward, and Thomas Watsons and one Charles Watson who have held various titles such as knight, baron, earl and marquess.

Today Rockingham Castle remains the private home of the Saunders-Watson family. According to James Saunders-Watson, "This remarkable castle, built on the instruction of William the Conqueror, has been my family's home for 450 years. Prior to the Watsons' ownership, the castle was held by the crown. There are very few other homes that have been continuously occupied for nearly 1000 years and within that time been owned by just one family since being relinquished as a royal castle." Tickets are available online for visits to the castle during the summer or for special events at the castle.

The surname Watson and other forms such as Wat, Watt, MacWattie, Macouat and MacWatson are of English and Scottish origin meaning "son of Wat," a common nickname for Walter from the Middle Ages. The surname Wat is first recorded in the Pipe Rolls of Devonshire in England in 1176 as "Peganus Wat." In Scotland the earliest recording is that of John Watson, who held lands in Edinburgh in 1392. A Robert "Watsoun" is recorded in Aberdeen in 1402 and Sir Donald "Watsone" was a church presbyter in the diocese of Moray in 1493. The name became more frequently found in the 16th century and is particularly frequent in the Lowlands and the North-East of Scotland. Wattie is found particularly in Aberdeen and its surrounding area, and in a fishing village in Banffshire some years ago, 225 out of 300 inhabitants had the name Watt.

The Webbs: Alexander, William, John Richard, John
11th, 10th, 9th and 7th great-grandfathers, Walker line

From the earliest days of the American colonies, our immigrant ancestors tended to arrive alone. It usually took at least two months to make the dangerous journey and many died aboard ship before arriving in the colonies.

The Webb family must have been a brave and hardy lot. Alexander Webb and Mary Wilson arrived in New England in 1626 with almost all of their sons, daughters and grandchildren. They were among the earliest colonists in Massachusetts, arriving even before founding of the Puritans' Massachusetts Bay Colony in 1628.

They moved to Cambridge and within a few years were part of the original settlers of Stamford and then Wethersfield, Connecticut. The Webbs used their existing wealth, proven merchant and trading skills and old world connections to secure their place in colonial America.

One son, John, remained in England, possibly to look after the affairs of the remains of the family land holdings in England. Historical records show that he was a member of the British military who arrived in America in 1636, perhaps sent to ensure compliance of the colonies to British rule. If this is the case, it could have been a very interesting situation, since other members of the family became an integral part of the Revolutionary War effort.

Another of Alexander's sons left the family in New England and sailed on to Norfolk, Virginia, with his wife and children. It is from this contrarian, William Webb, that our family descends.

According to a Webb family history:

William Webb came to America in 1629 and was a merchant in Norfolk, Virginia. He originally settled at the Isle of Pines and then died at Norfolk. From him, styled "The Merchant of Virginia," came the great southern branch of the Webb Family. One of his sons, James, moved to Richmond, Virginia . . . His place of residence for a while was Smithfield, Isle of Wight. He was a renowned shipbuilder and designer.

William Shakespeare's birthplace in Stratford, England. Abigale Webb was Shakespeare's grandmother.

The wealthy Webb family came from Stratford, Warwickshire, England, where they had important connections to the courts of both Henry VII and Henry VIII. In fact, in the 15th century, Sir John Alexander Webb II, Alexander's grandfather, lived for some time at Hampton Court, one of the palaces of

Henry VIII. The palace, in Richmond upon Thames, is open to the public. Sir John was a knight who served in the armies of both Henrys and the family was part of the nobility who were granted land in return for their military service.

If the town of Stratford sounds familiar, it's because it was the home of William Shakespeare. The Webb family had complicated ties to both the prominent Shakespeare and Arden families of Stratford. In fact, in the 16th century, Abigail Webb, a daughter of John Alexander Webb, married Richard Shakespeare and was the grandmother of William Shakespeare.

We have 10 generations of both Ardens and Webbs in our Walker family tree. Marriages between Webb and Arden family members led to some distinguished direct ancestors, including: Egbert and Aethelwulf, kings of Wessex in the eighth and ninth centuries; and Alfred the Great of Wessex and Ethelred, earl of Mercia, in the ninth and tenth centuries.

Information about some of these early kings is included in the profile of Robert Coleman. The Arden family is one of only three families in England that can trace it's lineage in the male line back to Anglo-Saxon times. According to historian Sir William Dugdale, the Arden family was "one of the first here in England, that in imitation of the Normans, assumed a surname," he and his descendants calling themselves de Arden after the royal forest of that name in which their property lay.

The Ardens Anglo-Saxon lineage is unique in England because, after the Norman Conquest in 1066, King William the Conquerer removed English landowners from their estates and gave their land to his companions who had helped him conquer England.

Sir John Alexander Webb II lived for some time at Hampton Court, one of the palaces of Henry VIII.

Places associated with the Webb and Arden families include Castle Bromwich, a village in Warwickshire that was the home in the 13th and 14th centuries of our direct ancestor, Sir Anselme Bromwich and his descendants. Park Hall was bought by Henry de Arden in 1373. The Park Hall Manor House was supposedly haunted and was demolished in the early 1970s. The hall was first mentioned in 1265, but this could have been a nearby moated timbered dwelling. Remnants of the hall, farm house and adjacent buildings, orchard and pond are still visible at the Park Hall Wildlife Reserve. The name lives on in Park Hall School, which is on the other side of the road.

Through the Webbs and Ardens, we are directly descended from dozens of prominent English families, especially those of Norman descent or who took the prefix "de" when they were required to have surnames after the Norman Conquest. The custom was to add "de," meaning "of," before the town or place where they lived to create a surname. The following is a list of Webb and Arden ancestors whose names you might encounter during a visit to the British Isles:

Sir Richard de Vernon acquired Haddon Hall in Derbyshire (above) in 1170. The Vernons owned and continued to add to the manor until the 16th century. The ruins of Tancarville Castle (left) are near the city of Lillebonne in France. It was first built by the Tancarville family in the 11th century. (See list of Webb and Arden ancestors on following page.)

Webb and Arden ancestors

11th century
Walter Giffard, Normandy, France
Gerald Flaitel, Normandy, France

12th century
Agnes Burton, Hampden, Buckingshire, England
Avice de Avenel, Derbyshire, England
Lady Maud de Balliol, Bidwell Manor, Northhamptonshire, England
Hugh de Beauchamp, Eaton, Befordshire, England
Sibyl de Boulogne, Lorraine, France
Aubrey Alberic de Dammartin, Ille de France
Anne de Dreaux, Kent, England
Gerard de Greinville, Buckinghamshire, England
Simon de Hampden, Hampden, Buckinghamshire, England
Lady Margaret de Knightley, Knightley Manor, Staffordshire, England
William de Malbank, Cheshire, England
Mathilda de Ponthieu, Rhone-Alpes, France
Lucie de Tancarville, Tancarville, Normandy, France
Phillippa de Trailly, Bedfordshire, England
Dionysia de Turberville, Oxfordshire, England
Hugh de Vernon, Normandy, France;
Emma Fitz Osbern, Normandy, France,
Raufe Grosvenor, Cheshire, England

13th century
Wouter de Aylesbury, England
Sir John Belknap, Buckinghamshire, England
William de Bruley, Aston Bruley, Worcestershire, England
Walter de Burgh, 1st Earl of Ulster, Connaught, Ireland
Isabel de Sancta-Fide, Buckinghamshire, England
Lady Alice de Seagrave, Buckinghamshire, England
Bryan Herdeley, Buckinghamshire, England
Margaret Keyes, Buckinghamshire, England

14th century and beyond
Richard de Clodshale, Warwickshire, England
Sir John Fitz Rogers, Kent, England
Christopher Tocker, Ireland
Elizabeth Whalesboro, Cornwall, England

Refugees

German: Johan Jurg and Johan Michael Meisser
6th and 7th great-grandfathers, Watson line

The Meissers are among some 13,000 Germans who emigrated from Germany to England between May and November 1709. The mass emigration was triggered by the promise of free land in the American colonies.

Towards the end of the 17th century and into the 18th, the wealthy Middle Rhine region (now Germany) was repeatedly invaded by French troops, which destroyed cities and created economic hardship for the people who lived in the region. On top of that, the winter of 1708 was one of the coldest in history. Vines and fruit trees were killed, which explained why free tenant farmers made up more than half of the emigrants.

Although the English didn't know it at the time, they learned late that several "agents" working on behalf of the Colony of Carolina had promised the peasants around Frankfurt free passage to the plantations. Spurred by reports of the success of a few families, thousands of German families headed down the Rhine to England and the New World.

As the first boatloads of refugees, nicknamed "Poor Palatines," began arriving in 1709, the English provided housing, food and supplies, and later settled them in fields of Army tents. Finding employment for them proved more difficult however, for unlike previous migrant groups—skilled, middle-class, religious exiles such as the French Huguenots or the Dutch in the 16th century—they were unskilled rural laborers, neither sufficiently educated nor healthy enough for most types of work.

When resettlement in Ireland for some of the emigrants proved mostly unsuccessful, the English began transporting them to the American colonies. Nearly 3,000 German Palatines in ten ships arrived in New York in 1710. Many of them were first assigned to work camps along the Hudson River to work off their passage. About 850 families settled in the Hudson River Valley. Others, after working off the cost of their passage, were the first Europeans to acquire land in present-day Herkimer County on both sides along the Mohawk River.

Johan Jurg Meisser's name was on the sixth embarkation list of German Palatines who were scheduled to sail from Holland for New York via England, on July 28, 1709, "with wrow & 4 kinder," according to Walter Allen Knittle in his book, *Early 18th Century Palatine Emigration*.

Jurg's son, 15-year-old Johann Michael Meisser, was among the "4 kinder" on the ship's list. He and his father are the only ones known to have survived the voyage. Names of Jurg's wife and other children do not appear in any historical records.

Although they were scheduled to embark in December 1709, the ship did not actually set sail until April 1710. They were on board the ship for six months before it arrived in New York in the summer of 1710. The ship was crowded, conditions were difficult and food was of the poorest quality. Out of about 3,000 immigrants, at least 470 had died during the voyage or soon after while they were housed in tents to recover from their illness and the effects of the voyage.

The Meissers were among the New York immigrants who worked off their passage in work camps along the Hudson River, then settled in Herkimer County and the Schoharie Valley. The immigrants believed the land had been given to them by Native leaders but they could not secure title because the Natives had already given the land away to other settlers. Because the Natives believed that no one really owned the land, they had nothing to lose by selling it or giving it away again.

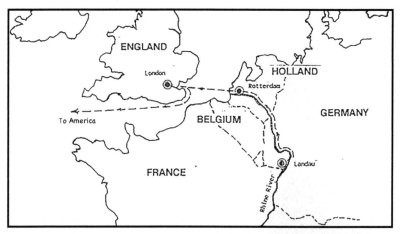

Some 13,000 Germans migrated to England between May and November 1709. They fled down the Rhine River to the Dutch city of Rotterdam, where the majority embarked for London and some on to America.

Michael Meisser married Anna Elizabeth Sixt in about 1723. This was the same year that Governor Keith of Pennsylvania invited the Germans to settle there. It seems that Michael and Elizabeth were married in New York and then set off as part of a group of 15 German Palatine families from the Scholharie Valley to travel to the Tulpehocken region in present Berks County, Pennsylvania. They floated down the Susquehanna in canoes, up the Swatara, then moved on the Tulpehocken, while driving their cattle over land.

The Palatines cleared, cultivated and improved the land, all without purchasing land from the Natives or others who may have claimed it. The settlers thought that they were legally entitled to the land, having been invited there by the governor of the commonwealth. The heirs of William Penn claimed that the land was theirs and the commonwealth had no

The home of Hans Zeller (above) was adjacent to the original land of Michael Meisser. Zeller's home, the strongest in the area, became known as Fort Zeller where all the settlers sought refuge against Indian attacks.

right to dispose of it. In the meantime, the settlers were joined by thousands of emigrants from Germany. An estimated 65,000 people landed in Philadelphia between 1727 and 1775. In time, the commonwealth and the Penns decided to settle with the immigrants as it was virtually impossible to evict them.

In 1731, Michael Meisser acquired land near Millbach in the Tulpehocken region through deed from Chief Allummapie and purchase from the Penns. The lands that Michael settled were passed to the eldest son of each successive generation, each of whom was named George Meiser, until the chain was broken when the land was acquired by a daughter of George S. Meiser by will in 1894.

The home of Hans Zeller was adjacent to the original land of Michael Meisser. Zeller's home, the strongest in the area, became known as Fort Zeller where all the settlers would seek refuge against attacks by Natives. This "fort" still stands, marked by a historical stone monument and bronze plaque. According to a Zeller family website, "Zeller's Fort is one of the few and rare remaining examples of Germanic architecture in the Western Hemisphere and is also Pennsylvania's oldest existing fort. Pioneers who came to the Tulpehocken from the Schoharie Valley built it in 1723 and rebuilt it in 1745. It was used as a place of refuge during Indian Wars."

Johan Jurg Meisser is believed to be the ancestor of every person with that surname living in the United States. The family of our closest ancestor, my grandmother, Eva Belle Miser, used the simplest spelling of the name. Other spellings include Meiser, Meisser, Meisel, Messor, Mesher, Masar, Messier, and many more.

The surname has several origins, including the occupational name for a person who hunts birds, the name for someone who lived in an area where timber was felled, or for someone from a place called Mais in Bavaria. It was first found in Austria, where the family aligned itself with nobles and princes during struggles for power and status in the region. It was found in England after the Norman Conquest. Roger Messer was the first on record in Lincolnshire in 1172. Jocobus Mesoart was registered in Normandy and a branch of the family relocated to Scotland. Some notable Meisers were Adolph von Meissel, who served as Lord Chamberlain to the Queen of Sweden, and Karl Meisl, a Viennese playwright.

Scot-Irish: Thomas Wallace
2nd great-grandfather, Walker line

Thomas Wallace and his family were among about 4.5 million Irish who arrived in America between 1820 and 1930. The 19th century migration was not the first from Ireland. During the 1700s, about 200,000 Protestants left Northern Ireland for the American colonies. Those early settlers helped some of the later migrants, including the Wallace family. A glimpse of Tom Wallace's younger years is recorded in a letter written in 1941 by Wallace descendant Thomas A. Bussong. According to Bussong:

> *Grand Ma Wallace came here in about 1840 & settled in Lebanon [St. Claire County in Southern Illinois] & came from Tuber Moore [Tobermor], County Derry Ireland. . . . She died in 1877 and was 82 yrs. old. Born about 1795 . . . She arrived here with 5 youngsters & like all good Scotch-Irish poor as a church mouse. She washed & done housework & the boys . . . was placed around with different farmers so as to take the green off. Dr. J. W. Peck a Bap. Missionary here helped them & got them going.*

Bussong went on to describe the lives of the children, including:

> *Uncle Tom Wallace went west during the Gold fever in 48 or 49. He dug Gold there & then bot a farm & died on it about 1878. Shingle Spring Calif. is their add[ress].*

Thomas Wallace married Sarah Tully, a descendant of Huguenot emigrant Peter Tuly. Sarah was born in Virginia, then resettled in Illinois with her family in about 1840. From Illinois, the Tullys traveled by covered wagon to California during the Gold Rush, where Sarah became one of the first school teachers in El Dorado County.

Thomas Wallace came from Tobermore in Northern Ireland.

We don't know how Sarah Tully and Thomas Wallace met. Sarah helped young miners who were unable to read and write manage their earnings from the mines.

It could be that Thomas was one of those she helped. Or they might have met in church—they both were Protestants and probably were associated with the Placerville Methodist Episcopal Church built in 1851. Burial records show that their youngest child is buried at the church.

We do know, though, that in about 1857, Thomas Wallace cashed in some of his earnings as a miner to buy a farm and marry the young schoolteacher. In 1860, Thomas purchased another 320 acres on Deer Creek in what now is El Dorado Hills, California.

The 1860 census reported the 25-year-old Thomas, a native of Ireland, was a farmer with real estate valued at $5,000 and personal worth of $3,100. His wife, Sarah, a native of Virginia, was 23 [should be 25], and they had a 3-year-old daughter, Maria. Also living with them were miners or farm workers from Ireland, Sweden, Norway, New York and Indiana. Apparently Sarah was adding to the family income not only by teaching but also by running a boarding house.

By the 1870 census, there probably wasn't much time for teaching or room for boarders. Thomas, 38, and Sarah, 36, now had seven children and Thomas' net worth had declined to $3,625 in real estate and $1,829 in personal worth. Two more children were born before Thomas died on January 15, 1886, at the age of 54. Most of his eight surviving children were grown and the older girls had married, but three younger children were still living at home.

The eldest daughter, Maria Louisa Wallace, continued the Walker line with her marriage to Frank X. Walker. Maria's brother, Charles T. Wallace, married my great-grandmother, Leontine Miller, after she divorced our great-grandfather, Joseph Miser.

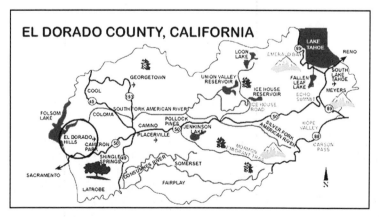

Tom Wallace's farm was on Deer Creek in Shingle Springs, in the area now known as Eldorado Hills.

The family must have been hit hard by Thomas' death. Sarah had to borrow money and neighbors chipped in to help pay for his funeral expenses. In 1901, she sold the Wallace farm for $3,500.

According to terms of the estate settlement, Sarah and the three youngest children were entitled to remain in the dwelling house on the Wallace land. The profits from the land sale were divided among Sarah and her grown children.

When Thomas Wallace and his family left Ireland, there were many Wallaces in the eastern part of Northern Ireland—105 households in County Derry alone. Many were descendants of Lowland Scots who first came to Northern Ireland in the early 17th century. They came as part of a state-sponsored scheme intended to confiscate all of the lands of the Gaelic Irish nobility in Northern Ireland and to settle the province with Protestant Scottish and English colonists. A second wave of Scottish immigrants to northern Ireland arrived in the late 1690s when tens of thousands of people fled a famine in Scotland.

Even before the Potato Famine of the mid-1800s, Ireland was a country of extreme poverty. Most people were desperately poor, with nearly half of families in rural areas living in windowless mud cabins with no more belongings than a pot and a stool.

These impoverished people depended on the potato as the main part of their diet. When the potato crop rotted from blight, the people began leaving to escape starvation. Census figures show an Irish population of 8.2 million in 1841, 6.6 million a decade later, and only 4.7 million in 1891.

Some Irish emigrants went to Great Britain and to Australia, but most intended to go to America. Many left dressed in rags with not enough food to last the 40-day journey across the Atlantic and not enough money to buy food sold on board. Many thousands died on the dangerous journey across the Atlantic.

According to Thomas Bussong's letter:

> *Our kind came from Scotland in days gone by & fought I think in the fight between Prod.[estants] & Cat.[holics]. I believe they figured in that battle of the Boyne . . ."* The Battle of the Boyne was fought in 1690 between two rival claimants of the English, Scottish, and Irish thrones—the Catholic King James and the Protestant King William across the River Boyne near Drogheda on the east coast of Ireland. The battle, won by William, was a turning point in James' unsuccessful attempt to regain

the crown and ultimately helped ensure the continuation of Protestant ascendancy in Ireland.

The Wallace family in Scotland is an ancient clan that first came to Scotland with the Norman Walter Fitz Alan. One of his followers was Richard Wallace, who came from Shropshire on the Welch border.

The Wallace surname may be a corruption of Le Waleis meaning "Welshman." Riccarton Castle, in Riccarton, Ayrshire, was named after Richard Wallace (Richard's Town). The lands were held by the Wallaces from the 13th century or earlier and they had a castle there. Malcolm Wallace, who is the father of the patriot William Wallace, is said to have been born there and a plaque now marks the site. Other castles with connections to the Wallace Clan include the ruins of Craigie Castle near Kilmarnock and Craigie

Historic places in Scotland associated with the Wallace Clan include, from top left:
- Craigie House in Ayrshire, built by Sir Thomas Wallace in 1730;
- Carnell House, originally "Cairnhill," in Ayrshire, built by the Wallace family in the 13th century;
- Wallace Tower Sundrum Castle in Ayreshire, built by Sir Robert Wallace in the 14th centuiry; and
- Ruins of Craigie Castle in Kilmarnock, built in the 12th century and occupied by members of the Wallace Clan from 1371 to 1588.

House, near Ayr, built by the Wallaces in 1730, now a part of Paisley University. Auchenbathie Tower near Beith is in ruins, Busbi Castle in Knockentiber was demolished in 1949, and Crosbie Castle near West Kilbride, Ayrshire, was demolished and set aside as a public park.

Wallace Tower Sundrum Castle was built in the 14th century by Sir Robert Wallace, sheriff of Ayr. The castle and its 85-acre estate is currently undergoing restoration. The 2000-acre Carnell Estate in Moss Side in East Ayrshire originally belonged to the Wallace family, ancestors of the present owners. The original 16th century tower built by the Wallaces still exists although the property has been extended and modernized since the mid-1800s. Today, both Sundrum Castle and Carnell House offer accommodations for private parties and conferences.

William Wallace, the clan's greatest hero, was a Scottish knight who became one of the main leaders during the Wars of Scottish Independence. He was appointed Guardian of Scotland and served until his defeat in 1298. In August 1305, Wallace was captured near Glasgow and handed over to King Edward I of England, who had him hanged, drawn, and quartered for high treason and crimes against English civilians. Wallace has been immortalized in literature and the 1995 Academy Award-winning film *Braveheart*. During our 2016 visit to the British Isles, we saw several tributes to him, including a statue at Edinburgh Castle, and in London, a plaque at St. Batholomew's Hospital marking the place where he was executed. The plaque reads:

To the Immortal Memory of Sir William Wallace, Scottish patriot born at Elderslie Renfrewshire circa 1270 AD who from the year 1296 fought dauntlessly in defence of his country's liberty and independence in the face of fearful odds and great hardship being, eventually betrayed and captured, brought to London and put to death near this spot on the 23rd August 1305. His example, heroism and devotion inspired those who came after him to win victory from defeat and his memory remains for all time a source of pride, honour and inspiration to his countrymen.

French Huguenots: Peter Tuly and Anthony Toncray

Tracing the origins of Huguenot ancestors is a challenging task. The 1818 wedding of James Tully and Dorcas Toncray in Abingdon, Virginia, offers some important clues to their Huguenot ancestry. First, they were married by the Presbyterian minister Rev. Stephen Bovell (originally Bouville), a descendant of French Protestants and popular member of the Virginia Huguenot community. The marriage took place at Sinking Springs Presbyterian Church. Presbyterianism grew out of the Calvinist tradition, as did the Reformed Church of France, and today is the largest Protestant denomination in France.

The Protestant Reformation had roots in England and France as early as the 14th century, when widespread corruption in the Catholic Church was exciting wars between princes and uprisings among the peasants. Beginning in the 1550s, the Reformation became a popular movement in France. The origin of the word Huguenot is unclear—it may have begun with the term for night spirits, "le Roy Huguet," used by priests mocking people who gathered secretly at night to study the Bible—but sometime between 1550 and 1580, members of the Reformed Church of France came to be commonly known by that name. Huguenot numbers grew rapidly after 1550, chiefly among nobles and city dwellers. From the outset of the Reformation, Huguenots faced persecution, as the Calvinist followers became known for their harsh criticisms of the doctrine and worship of the Catholic Church.

The religious tensions spurred a series of civil wars and Huguenots became organized as a definitive political movement. During the St. Bartholomew's Day massacre in October 1572, Catholics killed more than 30,000 Huguenots in Paris and other towns. A period of peace began in 1598, when Henry IV issued the Edict of Nantes, which granted Huguenot equality with Catholics under the throne and a degree of religious and political freedom.

Huguenot cross

All that ended in 1685 when Louis XIV revoked the Edict of Nantes and declared Protestantism to be illegal. The revocation forbade Protestant services, required education of children as Catholics and prohibited emigration. While it is estimated that about three-quarters of the Protestant population converted to Catholicism following the revocation, more than 200,000 illegally fled to different countries. In most cases, they escaped with only what they could carry. Their homes and families may have been decimated by wars so links to family histories are difficult to trace.

Aside from the time of their arrival in the American colonies, there is little in the way of solid historical facts to link the Tully and Toncray families to the French Huguenot emigration. However, family oral histories, letters and biographies seem to support the theory:

- *In December 1919, Alexander Toncray of Los Angeles, California, wrote in a letter: "So I will now try and enlighten you as to our origin, which was related to me by my father, who passed away in 1860. Records of the family having been lost, he told me that the original Toncray family came from Normandie, France, and spelled the name Tonquereax, which translated in pure U.S. is Toncray."*

- *Roscoe Goodcell was a grandson of Maria Louisa Tully and David Bennett. He wrote in a family history entitled* Our Early Years, *"Mother's side of the story, which is also lost in uncertainty, begins in France. Grandfather David was born in Lexington, Kentucky. His ancestors were Huguenots and had been driven out of France at the time of the revocation of the Edict of Nantes. They had found refuge in Holland and later came to South Carolina and then to Kentucky and Illinois. Grandmother Louise Tully (or Tulee) came from one of the old first families of Virginia. They, too, had been Huguenots and had also been expelled from France. Among these ancestors was Counte de Tonquene (I don't know the spelling) but who he was and what he did is apparently unknown to this generation."*
  [Note: Earl of Tankerville is a title drawn from Tancarville in Normandy which has been created three times, twice in the Peerage of England and once (in 1714) in the Peerage of Great Britain for Charles Bennet, 2nd Baron Ossulston. His father John Bennet, 1st Baron Ossulston, was the older brother of Henry Bennet, 1st Earl of Arlington. Bennetts continue to hold the Tankerville title to this day.]

- *William Floyd Tuley, in his book,* The Tuley Family Memoirs, *said, "The Tuley family's ancestors came to this country about two hundred and fifty years ago. They were French Huguenots, rather* descendants of those of that faith who fled to England after the St. Bartholomew Massacre in 1572. Three brothers named Tulé landed in South Carolina during the last quarter of the 17th Century. One of these went ot Louisiana, another up into New York State, and a third, Peter, located in Powhattan County, Virginia."

- *According to an article about McCall's, a historical place in Wythe County, Virginia, "The next family to become identified with this place was the Anthony Toncray family." At the sesquicentennial display of antiques, a descendant of Anthony Toncray presented an old hammer which had been handed down for generations by will. "Its interest lies in the fact that it was brought to America by the Toncray family, French Huguenots, who had fled from France about 1685. According to the legend, it was used in the building of the first tower clock to be built in America."*

Peter Tuly, 7th great-grandfather, Walker line
Peter Tuly was among French Huguenot refugees living in London who, in 1700, were promised land grants by the English Crown in Lower Norfolk County off Chesapeake Bay at the mouth of the James River. Many Huguenots were artisans and merchants who expected to settle near the Atlantic ocean where they could manufacture and export cloth and other trading goods.

When they arrived, Lt. Gov. Francis Nicholson defied orders of King William III and directed the immigrants to settle on the James River near Richmond—about 120 miles inland—at the abandoned Monacan tribe's village of Manakin Town. John Fontaine, a Huguenot descendant, claims that Nicholson cited confusion regarding the Virginia-North Carolina border as one reason for ignoring the

king's direction, but clearly William Byrd II, who had patented large tracts of land including the site of the city of Richmond, used his influence to ensure that the immigrants stayed in Virginia rather than ending up in North Carolina.

Lt. Gov. Nicholson supported Byrd's plan to use the Manakin Town settlement as a potential buffer between existing colonial settlements and the "threatening Natives" on the western frontier. According to historian James Bugg:

> *The falls of the James was in 1700 the last outpost of western settlement in Virginia. Between that point and the site of the Monocan Indian village lay some twenty-five miles of virgin and virtually trackless forests, a green and silent wall of loneliness which would separate the French from their closest neighbors . . .*

Although the danger from Natives was probably slight, for no tribe lived in the immediate neighborhood, the fear of possible plunder and murder died slowly. As late as June of 1702 the council ordered the Henrico County military officers to visit the "French settlement . . . once every week to charge them not to leave their habitation nor to straggle into the woods any distance from their settlements."

"Peter Tuly and his wife" are on a list of French refugees destined for Manakin Town. That list, subtitled "In ye first Shipp," also includes "John Farcy and his wife" and "Sublet and his wife and four children." These names further establish the Tully's as members of the Huguenot community, as Laura Tully, daughter of James and Dorcas Tully married Thomas Forsee, whose mother was a Sublett. Daughter Maria Louisa married David Bennett, a descendant of the South Carolina Huguenot immigrant, Jacques Benoit. This choice of marriage partners within the

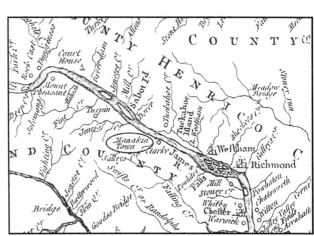

Virginia's Huguenot immigrants were directed to settle in an undeveloped area about 120 miles east of Jamestown.

Huguenot community supports a theory that French Huguenots who settled in homogeneous rural communities in New York, Virginia and South Carolina maintained more of their unique cultural identity and group preferences than those who settled in urban communities.

Peter Tuly was not included on later lists of residents of Manakin Town. While 207 immigrants had arrived on the first ship, the Mary Ann, only 120 accompanied William Byrd and soldiers into the forest for the journey to the settlement. A number of immigrants were too sick to travel further or left to join other settlements in Virginia, Maryland, the Carolinas and other colonies. Although the four ships that crossed the Atlantic in the summer and fall of 1700 and the winter of 1701 brought between 700 and 800 French Protestants to Virginia, only 390 of those went to Manakin Town.

The Huguenots of 1700 were not the first to arrive in Virginia. According to the Manakin Huguenot Society, Huguenots began coming to Virginia as early as 1620. French names appear in York County, the upper County of New Norfolk, Lower Norfolk, Princess Ann and Isle of Wight Counties. William F. Tuley mentions that a "Mr. Tuley (Christian name not given) was recorded as buried in 1668 in the Old Bristow Parish Churchyard at Williamsburg," which indicates that other Tuley/Tullys may have arrived earlier. A listing of 1704 rent rolls obtained by Lt. Gov. Nicholson from the English government included several Tullys: in Princess Ann County, Mark Tully, 300 acres, James Tully, 400 acres, and Thomas Tully, 600 acres; in Norfolk County, John Tully, 165 acres; and in New Kent County, William Tully, 200 acres. It is not known whether these individuals are related to Peter Tuly or are Huguenots.

Some researchers believe that Peter Tuly is the "Pierre Tillou" included among an ancestor listing by the Huguenot Society of South Carolina, a suggestion supported by the Tuley and Goodcell family histories. Although Peter's whereabouts after his arrival in Virginia are unclear, it is generally believed that he was the father of John Tuly, who founded the Tully line in Virginia.

Records show that Peter Tuly may have been born March 16, 1660, in Villegenon in the Centre region of France, near Sancerre, a city that played a key role in the history of the religious wars in France:

> Sancerre was the site of the infamous Siege of Sancerre (1572–1573) during the Wars of Religion where the Huguenot population held out for nearly eight months against the Catholic forces of the king. The siege

was one of the last times in European history where slings (trebuchet), the "Arquebuses of Sancerre," were used in warfare. The siege was documented by a Protestant minister who survived the battle, Jean de Léry, in The Memorable History of the Siege of Sancerre. In 1621 much of the feudal chateau and city walls were destroyed by orders of the king to prevent further resistance. In 1640 the county became the possession of the Prince of Condé, Henry II of Bourbon, the governor of Berry. The area suffered economically from the mass exodus of Protestant merchants, tradesmen and others during the 17th century, especially after the revocation of the Edict of Nantes (1685).

Peter Tuly's son, John Tuly, as a young man was overseer of Edward Scott's plantation near present day Scottsville, Virginia. He surveyed the road from the plantation to Rock Fish River in 1732. This was part of the old River Road. John Tuley's name survives on some of the old maps where Totier Creek is shown as Tooley's Creek. A Tooley's Hill is also mentioned in this area in the road orders of the 1790s. The River Road is the first documented road penetrating modern Albemarle County.

According to his will, by the end of his life John Tuly was a successful landowner who bequeathed land to each of his three sons and other property to his three daughters. He was married to Sarah New, daughter of Edmund New, and was brother-in-law to Watson ancestor Thomas Christian.

Anthony Toncray, 6th great-grandfather, Walker line
Anthony Toncray (or Antoine Tancre) was among thousands of French Protestants, or Huguenots, who escaped after King Louis XIV declared Protestantism illegal in France. We don't know where in France he was from or the host country he lived in between the time he left France and his journey to New York around the middle of the 18th century.

Because he came to New York, it is likely that Anthony was in the German Palatine. Between 1688 and 1714, the Palatine region became the center of deadly conflicts between the Protestant German state and France, devastating the region. The Palatines fled to England, which in turn sent them to help populate its North American colonies. Hundreds of English ships carried thousands of Palatines across the Atlantic between 1709 and 1775. The largest Palatine migration to New York was in 1709 and 1710, but because Anthony Toncray probably was not born until after 1710, he must have come during later migrations between 1727 and 1775.

Although New York was primarily settled by Dutch and German immigrants, there were several French Huguenot settlements in and near Dutchess County. The town of New Paltz in Ulster County, founded in 1678 by both patent and purchase from the local Esopus tribe, was settled by Huguenot refugees from Mannheim in the German Palatinate. They named the new town after die Pfalz, the region along the Rhine River where they had found temporary refuge before journeying to the new world. A neighborhood in New York City's borough of Staten Island is named Huguenot, and the city of New Rochelle in Westchester County is named after La Rochelle, a former Huguenot stronghold in France.

In 1750, Anthony Toncray and Samuel Rogers purchased two tracts totaling 5,400 acres in an area of Dutchess County known as the Oblong. The land was given to New York in 1683 to settle a long dispute with Connecticut over a 61,660 acre tract on the southwest corner of the state now known as the Connecticut Panhandle. In exchange, New York was granted the town of Rye in Westchester County as well as the 2 x 60-mile-wide strip along the Connecticut border known as the Oblong. The village of Pawling, located in the Oblong, played a role in the revolutionary war; General George Washington and his Continental Army encamped there in the winter of 1767.

We don't know how Anthony got the funds to purchase such a large piece of land. Most of the Palatine refugees were put into work camps where they were able to earn enough to build houses and purchase small farms. Anthony, however, must have had other sources of wealth to buy so much land. Many of the French Huguenot were wealthy merchants or craftsmen, so he may have been able to escape from France with some of his family's wealth.

In 1750, Anthony Toncray partnered to purchase two tracts totaling 5,400 acres in an area of Dutchess County known as the Oblong.

The population of Dutchess County was only a little more than 1,000 persons in 1722, but between 1749 and 1756, the population had increased to more than 14,000. Anthony Toncray married and contributed to the population increase by producing at least four, possibly more children during that time period. According to *Smith's History of Dutchess County*, "Wm. Tonkey came from France, and bought a large tract east of the center line of the Oblong, extending northward to Boston Corners. He had there sons, Daniel, Anthony, and Nicholas, and one daughter. They lived near the town of Northeast, in the north section of the Oblong."

In 1758, Toncray and Rogers sold all or part of the second tract of 3,100 acres. Anthony Toncray was named on Dutchess County tax lists from 1760 to 1779, his sons John in 1771, Daniel in 1790, Nicholas until 1821.

All of Anthony Toncray's sons served in the Revolutionary War. Quarter Master Daniel Toncray served under Lt. Colonel Henry Van Rensselaer in the Sixth Regiment, Fourth Rensselearwick Battalion. Anthony II served in Hatch's Company of Minute Men, and Nicholas was in Nicoll's Regiment of the Levies (Pawling).

Our Walker line descends from Anthony II, who made his way to Virginia soon after the war. His granddaughter, Dorcas Toncray, married James Tully, a second great-grandson of Huguenot immigrant Peter Tuly.

The Toncray name is believed to have derived from the name Tancre in France, which in turn was originally Tancred. The family is thought to have descended from the 10th century nobleman Tancred de Hauteville. Tancred had 12 sons, almost all of whom left Normandy for southern Italy and acquired some prominence there. Tancred, a 12th-century descendant, was a Norman leader of the First Crusade who later became Prince of Galilee and regent of the Principality of Antioch.

Tancred of Sicily was King of Sicily in the late 12th century. His death, at Palermo a few days after that of his young son and co-king, Roger III, opened the way for Henry IV, King of the Romans, to rule in Sicily.

Tancred de Hauteville sired 12 sons, most of whom gained fame and prominence in southern Italy.

In England, Brampton Hall, a farmhouse in Langthorpe, Boroughbridge, was for several generations the residence of the ancient family of the Tankards (Tancreds). In the 17th century, Sir Richard Tancred, was knighted by Charles II for his services and sufferings during the English Civil War between Parliament and the Crown.

Today, the surname Tancre is prominent in the regions of Diekirch, Luxembourg; Wallonie and Vlaaderen, Belgium; Nord-Pas-De-Calais, Normandy and Lorraine, France; North Dakota, USA; Calabria, Italy; and Bremen, Germany. The surname Tanqueray is most prominent in Normandy and Corsica, France. It is best known for Charles Tanqueray, the 19th century British distiller who founded Tanqueray gin. The surname Toncray exists only in the United States, primarily in Kentucky, Idaho, Oregon, Tennessee and Illinois.

Quakers: Harlan, Buffington, Francis, Duck, Oborn and Cooke
Our Quaker ancestors and their families came from England and Ireland in the late 1600s. All are directly related on our Watson line as 7th and 8th great-grandparents.

While I was researching my Watson family immigrant ancestors, I was surprised to find a cluster of pious Quaker families among them. Most of our Watson line migrated to the American colonies for economic reasons, aligning themselves with the English Crown and the Church of England more for political convenience than religious devotion.

Friends' service organizations have used a red and black star as their symbol since the late 19th century.

As I studied our Quaker ancestors, I was even more surprised to find that they were the link to our Native ancestors. How did that happen? I'll explain later, but first here is some information about the Quakers.

The Quaker, or Friends, movement began in England in about 1650 when dissenting Protestant groups were breaking away from the politically powerful Church of England. The Quakers held new concepts of family and community and offered leadership roles for women. Members were called Quakers because they were said "to tremble in the way of the Lord." They believe that there is something of God in everybody. They do not have clergy or rituals and their meetings for worship are often held in silence, although any member may speak at any time during the meeting.

Quakers believe in the universal priesthood of all believers rather than through priests and bishops. Of course the hierarchical and male-dominated structure of the Church of England considered Quaker beliefs to be a blasphemous challenge to social and political order in England.

Our Quaker ancestors, the Harlans, Buffingtons, Oborns and their kin, are linked through the marriage in 1706 of Ezekial Harlan Sr. and Ruth Buffington, who both were brought to Pennsylvania as children. Ezekial was the son of George Harlan and Elizabeth Duck, who had first relocated their family from Durham, England, to County Down in Northern Ireland in 1678. In 1687, they sailed to America at the invitation of William Penn, who had established Pennsylvania as an American commonwealth run under Quaker principles.

The Buffington line goes back to Richard Buffington, who was in Pennsylvania in 1676, before William Penn was granted land there. Richard, who was Constable of Chichester, Delaware County, Pennsylvania, in 1689, was married three times and had 13 children.

Above, William Penn established Pennsylvania as an American commonwealth run under Quaker principles in 1681. Below, Benjamin Franklin, in his *Pennsylvania Gazette*, wrote about Richard Buffington's 60th birthday party on May 30, 1739.

Benjamin Franklin's paper, the *Pennsylvania Gazette*, reported that, on May 30, 1739, Richard's family gathered at his home to celebrate his 85th birthday. According to the report, "the children, grandchildren and great-grandchildren to the number of 115 met together at his house in Chester County. In addition to the blood descent, there were 9 sons-in-law and daughters-in-law and 12 great-grandchildren. His eldest son, (Richard, Jr.) now in the 60th year of his age was the first born of English descent in this province." Richard Buffington Sr. died in Chester in 1748.

Ezekiel and Ruth Harlan lived their married lives at Kennett Township, Chester County, where all their children were born. Their births are listed in the records of the Kennett Meeting House of Friends.

The Kennett Meeting House, now on the National Historic Register, was erected initially in 1710 on land previously granted by William Penn to Ezekiel Harlan. The area to become known as Kennett Square was originally inhabited by the Lenape Natives. The town was originally called Kennett Square, with the name "Kennett" coming

The Kennett Meeting house, now on the National Historic Register, was constructed in 1710 on land owned by Ezekiel Harlan, deeded from William Penn.

from the River Kennet in Berkshire, England, and "Square" coming from the original land grant from William Penn of one square mile. It was the site of General William Howe's march to the Battle of Brandywine during the American Revolution. Many of its prominent citizens helped slaves escape to the North for freedom as a part of the Underground Railroad. In 1853, a group asked for Kennett Square to be incorporated, and by 1855 it held elections.

Kennett Square's Quaker founders are credited with introducing mushroom growing to the area. They grew carnations, a popular local commodity around 1885, and wanted to make use of the wasted space under the elevated beds. They imported spores from Europe and started experimenting with mushroom cultivation. Today Kennett Square is known as the Mushroom Capital of the World because mushroom farming in the region produces over a million pounds of mushrooms a week. Half of America's mushrooms are grown in this tiny corner of southeastern Pennsylvania, which celebrates its heritage with the annual Kennett Square Mushroom Festival.

Quakers have been a significant part of the movements for the abolition of slavery, to promote equal rights for women, and peace. They have also promoted education and the humane treatment of prisoners and the mentally ill through the founding or reforming of various institutions. Quaker entrepreneurs played a central role in forging the Industrial Revolution, especially in England and Pennsylvania.

Regarding the connection between our Quaker and Native ancestors, I first thought it probably was related to Quakers who served as missionaries among the Natives who had been relocated to reservations west of the Mississippi River. I soon learned that the marriage in Tennessee between Ellis Harlan, grandson of immigrant Ezekiel Harlan Sr., and Ka Ti "Catherine" Kingfisher, the daughter of two prominent members of the Cherokee Nation, had little to do with Ellis' roots in the Quaker religion.

In fact, it seems that Ellis Harlan was not all that committed to his Quaker community's strict code of conduct. In 1764, he was formally disowned by the Chester County Friends for having given way "to his own Evil Inclinations, so far as to drink strong Liquor to Excess, and suffered his passion to rise so high as to Strike Several persons."

Renounced by his community, Ellis went south and became a trader among the Cherokee. During the Revolutionary War, the British took Ellis prisoner. While he was being held, the Tories and their Cherokee allies seized some of Ellis' property, for which he was never paid. Despite this dispute, according to historical papers, we know Ellis Harlan in 1777 already was much at home with the Cherokees, and seemingly trusted by whites and Natives alike.

When the Transylvania Company and the Cherokees held a great council fire at Sycamore Shoals on March 17, 1775, to consider a sale of Cherokee land, Ellis Harlan was one of the white traders present to act as an unofficial interpreter for the Cherokees and see that the official interpreter furnished by the Transylvania Company truthfully translated the term offered by the white promoters.

Ellis Harlan fathered a daughter with a Cherokee woman before marrying Catherine Kingfisher in 1786, with whom he had six children. Catherine was a daughter of Chief Kingfisher Walker and Nancy Ward, a Beloved Woman of the Cherokee Nation. As a Beloved Woman, Nancy Ward was allowed to sit in councils and to make decisions, along with the chiefs and other Beloved Women. Nancy is renowned in American history because of her efforts to achieve peaceful coexistence with the European-Americans and helping her people as a peace negotiator and ambassador.

California Swiss

Frank X. Walker
Great-grandfather, Walker line

Francis Xavier Walker's beginnings in the tiny village of Gurtnellen, Canton Uri, Switzerland, could not have foretold of his success in the ranching business in California. In 1881, the 21-year-old left his mountain village to make his way to the booming state of California. He was among several countrymen that Swiss immigrant and rancher Anton Russi imported to help with his expanding ranching and dairy business in Clarksville, near Sacramento.

Frank worked for Anton on his ranch and dairy farm until Anton's unexpected death in 1891 at age 46. Frank stayed on at the ranch and a year later married Anton's widow, Maria Louisa Wallace Russi. With Lou, he not only gained a spirited wife and successful ranching business, but also a ready-made family of five Russi children living at home. By 1900, three Walker children, Tom, Gene and Agnes, had joined the family.

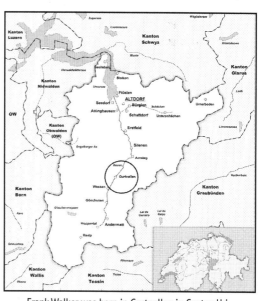

Frank Walker was born in Gurtnellen in Canton Uri, in the Swiss Alps near the center of Switzerland.

Frank showed himself to be a shrewd businessman, expanding the Russi's holdings to 2,800 acres in Clarksville and 3,500 acres in Blackwood Canyon, near Tahoe City, filling the pastures with up to 800 head of cattle bearing Frank's brand, the single letter X, for the Lone X Ranch.

Frank X. Walker's success at ranching was eventually undermined by his oldest son, my grandfather, Tom Walker. Management of the family ranches passed to him around 1920. It was a smooth transition at first, but the underlying economics of cattle ranching eventually unraveled for Tom Walker. With Sacramento beginning its eastward sprawl, Clarksville ranchers began selling their pastures to developers for a handsome profit. But Tom Walker never realized any of those gains. By the time local ranches were being bought up to create the sprawling residential community of El Dorado Hills in the late 1950s, the Walkers had been off their land for over 20 years.

Walker descendants disagree about where Tom Walker went wrong, but generally hold that he was never the same after his first wife died. The Great Depression surely played a part. Tom Walker's sister, Agnes Walker Shinn, told historian Melinda Peak that her brother Tom mismanaged the family ranch and lost it to creditors in the late 1930s. His daughter, Pat Johnson, recalls him being a good rancher, but poor with financial matters.

The Saga of Lake Tahoe, a comprehensive telling of the region's history, lays blame on family members who convinced Walker to forgo cattle for sheep, resulting in "financial suicide." The Walker ranch in Clarksville ended up in the hands of the Faustino Silva family, who only lived there a brief time, but nonetheless got their name on the prominent El Dorado Hills road which borders Serrano, while the Walker name faded into history.

Frank Walker's family history in Gurtnellen, Switzerland, is outlined in an extraordinary book known as the *Stammbuch von Uri.* This "book of citizens" is a hand-written record of family histories in Canton Uri, Switzerland, from the 1400s to early 1900s.

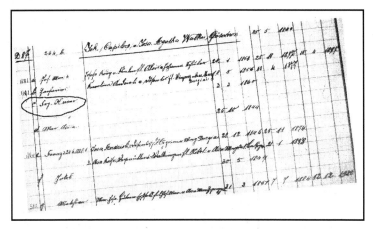

Frank Walker and his family's entry in the *Stammbuch von Uri*, a record of family histories in Canton Uri, Switzerland, from the 1400s to early 1900s. He is listed as "Fnz Xavier 3-3-1860."

Each record contains the father's name and often what village he was from, the wife's name including maiden name and their marriage date. After that, children of the marriage are listed, giving name, date of birth and marriage along with the spouse's name and parents. With the help of a numbering system, the lines are easily followed through generations. Families are arranged (roughly) alphabetically by surname, and chronologically (marriage date) within a surname.

The *Stammbuch* lists Francis Xavier Walker and six brothers and sisters under his parents, "Johann Walker, b. 1818, Gapil; m. Josefina Agatha Walker." Gapil refers to a street name in Gurtnellen, still shown on maps of the town to this day. Frank's family is among 10 generations of Walkers, each outlined in similar fashion, dating back to Peter Walker, the first Walker in Gurtnellen.

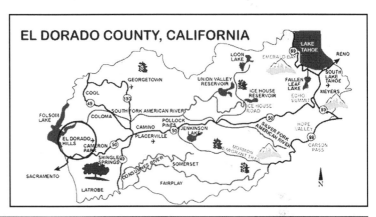

The Walker ranch, photographed in 1993 (below), was in Clarksville in an area now known as El Dorado Hills. The ranch site now is a shopping center.

Sometime before 1500, Peter Walker walked more than 200 miles through the Swiss Alps from Wallis (or Valais, the French pronunciation), a canton in southwest Switzerland, to Canton Uri. A note on the first page of the Walker section of the *Stammbuch* says "Peter Walker brought this company [his family] from Wallis to Silenen, and in the year 1500 bought land rights in Uri [Gertnellen] for 1111 gld. [gold?] for himself and his descendants. All of the Walkers in the district Uri are descended from this Peter."

As of 1929, when the record keeping ended, there were 624 Walkers in Canton Uri, one of the largest families in the registry. When Frank X. Walker went to California in 1881, he left a family that had been in the same place for ten generations—about 350 years—living in neighborhoods within an area of less than one square mile.

The original *Stammbuch* is kept in the Uri State Archive but microfiche images are available through Family History Centers located at LDS churches throughout the world. Anyone who may be interested in tracing their family in the *Stammbuch* should be aware that the book is written in German and an antique handwritten script. Although I was able to follow the numbering system, I had to enlist a translator to help me decipher the listings.

The book doesn't explain why Peter Walker left Canton Wallis to settle in Gurtnellen, but it's not hard to understand why his family remained there for so many generations. Gurtnellen is a beautiful village on the Gotthard Pass. It is near Goschenen, the site of the northern end of the Gotthard Tunnel, which opened in 1980 and connects German-speaking northern Switzerland and Italian-speaking southern Switzerland.

All of Switzerland is known for its breathtaking beauty, but the area along the Gotthard Pass is so spectacular it is almost beyond description. Tiny towns like Gurnellen that have clung to the mountainsides for centuries have carefully maintained architecture that reflects the area's historic past. As one travel blogger describes the landscape, "riding the train between major cities gives you some of the best views you could ever hope for. Mountains, valleys, lakes, rivers; I can understand why their tourism motto is 'Get Natural.'"

Switzerland is one of the most unique countries in the world. A team of enthusiastic Swiss bloggers at MySwissAlps.com suggest there are three things you must know about the history of Switzerland:

- *Switzerland was founded on August 1, 1291. August 1 is still the national holiday;*
- *Switzerland declared itself a neutral state in 1515. Neutrality still plays a major role in today's politics;*
- *Switzerland is a United Nations member since 2002. It still is not a European Union member.*

What this says to me is that the Swiss have a love and respect for their country's history, political neutrality and independence—characteristics I can see reflected in Frank Walker's descendants today.

From the mid-1800s, a good-sized Swiss immigrant community already was gathering in northern California. Most went into agricultural businesses, including dairy farming, ranching and the wine industry.

One of the first Swiss immigrant settlers was John Sutter, who is remembered for Sutter's Mill, where gold was first found in California in 1848. His property was not far from what later became the Walker Ranch. Sutter arrived in 1840 with a plan to establish a colony in the Sacramento area. After news of gold spread, large crowds of people overran his land and destroyed nearly everything Sutter had worked for.

To avoid losing everything, Sutter deeded his remaining land to his son John Augustus Sutter Jr. The younger Sutter, who had come from Switzerland and joined his father in September 1848, saw the commercial possibilities of the land and promptly started plans for building a new town. John Sutter wanted the town to be named Sutterville, but his son named it Sacramento, after the Sacramento River. Sacramento is now the capital of California and the fastest growing big city in the state.

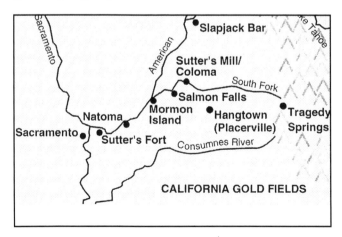

Sutter's Mill, where gold was first found in California, was about 20 miles from the Walker Ranch.

CHEROKEES

Sarah Emaline Beatty, my great-grandmother, is our family's link to the Cherokee Nation. She was married to Theodore Wigfall Watson in 1884 and bore him three daughters and my grandfather, Walter Earl Watson, born in 1892. Sarah died that same year, likely in childbirth, as did so many young women of her time. The children were raised by a stepmother.

Until recently, I knew nothing but the name of Sarah Beatty Watson. Then, as often happens on ancestry.com, a leaf signaling an ancestry hint appeared by her name. I clicked on the hint and learned that Sarah was a daughter of Emaline Parris and William Crawford Beatty. Further research revealed that both her Parris and Beatty lines contained prominent figures from the history of the Cherokee Nation. Emaline Parris was a daughter of Moses Parris, a leader among both the Eastern and Western Cherokee Nations. William Beatty was a great-grandson of Ellis Harlan (see "Quakers" in Refugees chapter), a 2nd great-grandson of Cherokee Chief Kingfisher Walker and Cherokee Beloved Woman Nancy Ward, and a descendant of the powerful Moytoy line of Cherokee chiefs.

Amatoya Moytoy, *8th great-grandfather, Watson line*
Amatoya Moytoy (pronounced mah-tie) was a Cherokee chief in the area of present-day Tennessee. His father, Thomas Pasmere Carpenter, was from the noble Anglo-Norman family of Vicompte Guillaume de

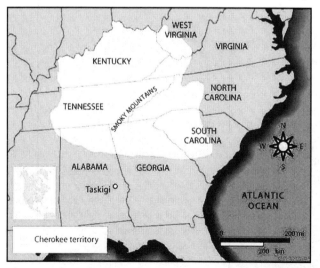

Before European settlement, the Cherokee Nation ranged from the Appalachian Mountains to the Mississippi River, and from the Ohio River to the Piedmont of present-day Georgia and Alabama, an estimated area of 100,000 square miles.

Melun le Carpentier, who descended from French kings and ancestors of the current British royal family. The Carpenter family owned sailing ships which served the English colonies in Virginia and Barbados.

Thomas Carpenter came to Jamestown in 1627. At age 20, he was too young to acquire a land grant, so lived in a cave near the Shawnee tribe and married a Shawnee woman. The tribe was driven out of Virginia by the Iroquois tribe and allowed to settle in Cherokee territory. Thomas' son, Trader Carpenter, called Ama Matai, Amatoya or Moytoy, became the first of a long line of Cherokee chiefs who ruled during the 18th and 19th centuries in the area now known as Tennessee.

Nancy "Nan'yehi" Ward, 6th great-grandmother, Watson line

Nancy Ward, who was a granddaughter of Chief Moytoy, was a Beloved Woman of the Cherokee, a designation that means that she was allowed to sit in councils and to make decisions, along with the chiefs and other Beloved Women.

The Cherokee were a matrilineal society, tracing their family relations through the mother. Women had great influence over family life, and those who showed extraordinary leadership were known as "Ghigau" or Beloved Women, the highest role a Cherokee woman could aspire to. Nan'yehi earned her title by fighting alongside her warrior husband, Kingfisher, against their enemy, the Creeks. During the fighting, Kingfisher was killed. Nan'yehi, about 18 years old at this time, took up her slain husband's gun and, singing a war song, led the Cherokees in a decisive victory over their enemy.

It was unusual for one as young as Nan'yehi to be named Ghigau, but since the name also translates as "War Woman" and was usually awarded to women warriors (or warriors' mothers or widows), Nan'yehi had duly earned it. Much responsibility went with the many privileges of the rank, and although young, Nan'yehi showed herself capable.

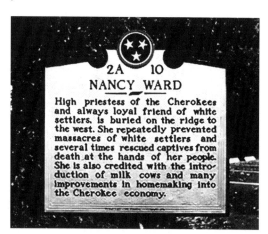

Nan'yehi could speak and vote in the Cherokee General Council and served as leader of the Women's Council. Another of her duties was to serve as an ambassador, or peace negotiator, with other tribes and English settlers on Cherokee lands. When militant Cherokees prepared to attack white settlements, Nan'yehi warned the settlers in time for them to defend themselves or flee.

One of the settlers taken alive by the Cherokee warriors was a young woman named Mrs. Bean. Nan'yehi rescued her as she was being prepared for execution, took her into her home and nursed her back to health. From Mrs. Bean, Nan'yehi learned how to weave cloth for

clothing, to raise dairy cattle and to prepare and use dairy foods, which would sustain the Cherokee when hunting was bad.

While these skills made the Cherokee people less dependent on traders, it also Europeanized them in terms of gender roles. While women had been responsible for tending the fields, men now became farmers and women became "housewives." It also led to use of slave labor among the Cherokee.

Although it might appear that Nan'yehi was encouraging the Cherokee people to adopt the European way of life, her political efforts

A sculpture of Nancy Ward (above) was stolen from her gravesite in Tennessee in the 1970s. It was found but as yet has not been returned. Her grave near Benton, Tennessee, is marked with a stone monument and a plaque donated by the local chapter of the Daughters of the American Revolution. The monument is next to those of her son, Fivekiller, and her brother, Longfellow.

proved she was ready to defend her people and her homeland against the advancing sea of European settlement on Native lands.

Nan'yehi, who became known as Nancy among non-Natives she befriended, hoped to avoid war but refused to compromise if she felt it would hurt her people. In 1781, she entered peace talks with a Tennessee politician and instructed him to take the treaty back to "his women" for them to ratify. It didn't occur to her that women didn't decide matters of war and peace in the white man's world. Nancy also was a negotiator for the Cherokees at the 1785 signing of the Treaty of Hopewell, the first treaty the Cherokees made with the United States.

By the early 1800s, it was becoming clear that the American lust for land could force her people off their homelands and destroy their way of life. As leader of the Women's Council of 1808, Nan'yehi urged her people to not sell their land to Americans, an appeal that she continued until her death in 1824.

Nancy became Nancy Ward when she married Scots-Irish trader Bryant Ward. Together they opened an inn near her birthplace in Chota in eastern Tennessee.

Nancy Ward was the last woman to be given the title of Beloved Woman until the late 1980s. She continues to be a powerful symbol for Cherokee women and is often referred to as an inspiration by feminist scholars.

Moses "Tu-Lu-Squit" Parris, 3rd great-grandfather, Watson line
Moses Parris was born in the Cherokee Nation in an area that later became Forsythe, Georgia. The Cherokee Nation in those days ranged from the Appalachian Mountains to the Mississippi River, and from the Ohio River to the Piedmont of present-day Georgia and Alabama, an estimated area of 100,000 square miles.

The Cherokees held the whole mountain region of the south Alleghenies, in southwest Virginia, western North Carolina and South Carolina, north Georgia, east Tennessee, and northeast Alabama, and claimed even to the Ohio River. It is estimated that about 30,000 to 35,000 people were living in the Nation in the 1600s and early 1700s, although communicable diseases brought by Europeans had killed as many as half of the Native population.

Moses' father, George (known as "Indian George") Parris, was the son of Capt. Richard Pearis, born in Ireland in 1725, whose family had settled in the Shenandoah Valley of Virginia when Richard was 10. By 1750, Capt. Pearis owned 1,200 acres of land near Winchester, where he lived with his wife and three children. He was a trader with the Cherokee Nation and operated a trading post in Tennessee. During the French and Indian War, Capt. Pearis led a company of Cherokee warriors who helped to retake Fort Duquesne. He later served as an agent among the Natives in Maryland.

During his time among the Cherokee, Capt. Pearis lived with a Cherokee woman named Pratchey. Pratchey may have been a member of the family of Moytoy chiefs. Richard Pearis and Pratchey had two daughters in addition to their son George. It's possible that Pratchey was a captive and slave, as one source cites a will in which Richard Pearis assigns Pratchey to his daughter Margaret.

George Parris was born in 1758 in Bedford County, Virginia, but at some point came to live among his Cherokee relatives in Georgia. He changed the spelling of his last name to Parris, possibly to differentiate from the Virginia George Pearises. George's son Moses Parris was born in 1784.

Many members of the Cherokee Nation in what now is Georgia were educated and had adopted the culture of the English settlers, becoming farmers and attending Protestant churches. Missionaries set up schools in the Native communities and by the 1820s, the Cherokees had a higher rate of literacy than the whites around them in Georgia.

Moses and George Parris were Presbyterians and, in 1818, they wrote to Presbyterian missionaries in the area to request a school near their homes. "We have agreed for you to teach school for us Natives here in this settlement we want you to commence as quick as possible we want our children to Learn. We

One of the first editions of the bilingual newspaper, *Cherokee Phoenix*, the first Native newspaper.

want you to pick out the place to set your School house." The Presbyterians wrote back that since the Baptists preached in that area, they should contact them.

As it turns out, the Parris family and others set up a private school, under no auspices of any church and hired an instructor from Georgia. This may have been Duncan O'Bryant, who taught in schools in Dawson and Cherokee counties from 1821 to 1831. During that time O'Bryant was ordained as a Baptist pastor and founded the Tinsawattee Baptist Church. It had approximately 30 members, including the Parris family, and Moses Parris was the only known deacon of the church.

Moses Parris appears to have been Duncan O'Bryant's right hand man. A visiting church leader reported, "One (member) is an excellent Interpreter. It is said he can, (and often does) get up after a sermon is delivered at length in English, and give it almost entire to his countrymen, in their native tongue, very impressively." When O'Bryant was too sick to speak, "brother Parris (our deacon) exhorted in Cherokee..."

In 1827, Moses Parris was a delegate to a convention in which the Cherokee Nation drafted a constitution modeled on the United States, with executive, legislative and judicial branches and a system of checks and balances. A printing press was established at New Echota and the tribe translated the Bible into Cherokee syllabary. The first edition of the bilingual *Cherokee Phoenix,* the first Native newspaper, was published in February 1828.

Moses Parris had this letter published in the *Cherokee Phoenix* in 1831, "I understand that some person has taken the unwarrantable liberty of putting my name down as one willing to take a reservation and come under the laws of Georgia. I hereby inform the public that I have never put my name down for such a purpose, nor authorized any person to do it."

Early in 1832, facing hostility from President Andrew Jackson and land-hungry Georgians following the Indian Removal Act of 1830, Moses Parris, Duncan O'Bryant, their families and about 28 members of the congregation headed for "the Arcansaw Contary."

They joined a larger traveling party headed for the territory that is now in eastern Oklahoma. The emigration group arrived in Arkansas at Fort Smith in May 1832 and within a month moved to Piney, Adair County, Oklahoma. The emigrants expected to be paid upon their arrival, but the western agent knew nothing about this arrangement. The agent who had arranged and led their travel also had miscalculated the amount of provisions needed for the emigrants, because he counted the slaves as property and not as people to be fed.

Moses Parris already was disliked by the Eastern Cherokees for serving as an interpreter for federal officials, and his move was viewed by the vast majority as being treasonous, temporarily impeding efforts among Native nationalists who defied state and federal authority over the Cherokee Nation.

Only a fraction of the Cherokees left voluntarily. Under orders from President Jackson, the U.S. government, with assistance from state militias, forced more than 16,000 remaining Cherokees west in 1838. The Cherokees were temporarily remanded in camps in eastern Tennessee. In November, they were broken into groups of around 1,000 each and began the journey west. They endured heavy rains, snow, and freezing temperatures. More than 4,000 of the relocated Cherokees died before reaching their destinations in the march remembered as the "Trail of Tears."

Apparently Moses Parris was forgiven by the Cherokee people because he went on to hold many important positions among the Western Cherokees. He represented his district during the Cherokee National Convention to sign the Act of Union between the Eastern and Western

Cherokees. He also was a signer of the Constitution and Laws of the Cherokee Nation, was elected senator to represent his district and later served as a member of the district council.

Moses was appointed as an associate justice of the Supreme Court of the Cherokee Nation and later as circuit judge for the Southern Circuit of the Cherokee Nation. He continued to take a leading role in his church, and was elected as vice-president of the Cherokee Bible Society. In 1860, he was elected clerk of the newly organized Convention of Churches in the Cherokee Nation, representing the New Echota Baptist Church in Adair County.

Bibliography

Some of these resources and others are included with ancestor profiles on ancestry.com.
Watson Family Tree: https://www.ancestry.com/family-tree/tree/33134704/family
Walker Family Tree: https://www.ancestry.com/family-tree/tree/15313302/family

Virginians

Crosley, Hillary, "When Were Blacks Truly Freed from Slavery?", The Root, www.theroot.com, 6/15/12
Egloff, Keith and Deborah Woodward: *First People: The Early Indians of Virginia.* Charlottesville: The University Press of Virginia, 1992.
Haile, Edward Wright (editor): *Jamestown Narratives: Eyewitness Accounts of the Virginia Colony: The First Decade: 1607-1617.* Chaplain: Roundhouse, 1998.
Jamestown Rediscovery, Historic Jamestown, http://historicjamestowne.org/history/virginia-company/
Keegan, John (2009): *The American Civil War.* New York: Alfred A. Knopf.
Kelso, William M. and Beverly Straube. "Jamestown Rediscovery 1994-2004." Association for the Preservation of Virginia Antiquities, 2004.
McCartney, Martha W.: *Jamestown: An American Legacy.* Hong Kong: Eastern National, 2001.
Price, David A.: *Love and Hate in Jamestown: John Smith, Pocahontas, and the Start of a New Nation.* New York: Alfred A. Knoff, 2003.
Salmon, E. J., & Salmon, J.: "Tobacco in Colonial Virginia." (2013, January 29). Encyclopedia Virginia, http://www.EncyclopediaVirginia.org/Tobacco_in_Colonial_Virginia.
Wood, Karenne (editor): "The Virginia Indian Heritage Trail." Charlottesville: Virginia Foundation for the Humanities, 2007.

Francis and Agnes Barrett
Agnes Mary Barrett New: https://www.findagrave.com/cgi-bin/fg.cgi?page=gr&GRid=101255407
Belhus, Essex: https://en.wikipedia.org/wiki/Belhus,_Essex
Bennett, John: *17th Century, Isle of Wight County, Virginia: Land Grants, 1628-1674,* http://genealogytrails.com/vir/isleofwight/land_grants_1628_1674.html
Huddleston, Roy H.: "Captain John Huddleston of the Bona Nova," http://freepages.genealogy.rootsweb.com/~virginiahuddlestons/captain_john_huddleston_of_the_b.htm
Morrison, Col. E.M.: "A Brief History of Isle of Wight County, Virginia," http://www.iwchs.com/IWCHistory.html

William Black
Magazine of History & Biography [PMHB], Vol. I, page 117)
Matthews, C.M.: *Barrett Origins, English Surnames,* (1966)

William and Mary Bostick
Mylius, Virginia Sanders, "Our Southern Cousins: Bostick Family," http://oursoutherncousins.com/bostick.html

Bostick, Joe: "Bostick Plantation," http://uspmobisites.com/bostick/joe-bostick/
McLellan, Jane, and Bostock, Tony, A History of a Village and Its People, http://www.bostockparishcouncil.gov.uk/bostock-a-history-of-a-village-its-people/

Giles Carter
Burnett, W.H.: "Vikings and Virginians: Giles Carter (1634-1701) of Henrico County (Turkey Island)"; http://www.vikingsandvirginians.com/2015/05/18/giles-carter-1634-1701-of-henrico-county-turkey-island/
Carter, William Giles Harding: *Giles Carter of Virginia: Genealogical Memoir.* Baltimore, Lord Baltimore Press, 1909.
"Our Maternal Carter Ancestors": http://freepages.genealogy.rootsweb.ancestry.com/~tqpeiffer/Documents/Surnames/MMPS/Carter/Carter%20MMPS.htm
Henrico Co. Records 1677-1691, p 303) Vol. 3, p 1380

Thomas Christian
Christian, William: *Christian Family of Virginia*, Richmond, Virginia 1921
"The Christian Family," *William and Mary College Quarterly, Vol. V*, pp. 261-263
The Chronicle of Man and the Sudreys, http://www.isle-of-man.com/manxnotebook/manxsoc/msvol22/index.htm
"Green Oak Farm," *William and Mary College Quarterly, Vol. VIII*, p. 70, April 1897
Harrison, William: "Illiam Dhône and the Manx Rebellion, 1651." Publications of the Manx Society (Vol. XXVI). Douglas, Isle of Man: Manx Society. (1877)
O'Dell, Jeff: letter describing Green Oak Farm published in the *Architectural Historian for the State of Virginia*, Sept. 18, 1991
Virginia County Records, VII, Henrico County, Book No. 11, p. 47

William Peter Christian
Family history document with quotes from many Cass County, Texas, Christian family descendants; Cass County Genealogical Society; p. 51
United States Federal Census Reports, 1840, 1850 1860, 1870, ancestry.com

John Coffey
Dictionary of American Family Names ©2013, Oxford University Press
Paul, D. Maria, "Cobhtaigh of Ancient Ireland," https://www.facebook.com/notes/cobhthaigh-coffey-clan/cobhthaigh-of-ancient-ireland/10150383664938517
Robertson, William (1889), *Historical Tales of Ayrshire*, Pub. Glasgow & London.
Way, George and Squire, Romily. (1994). *Collins Scottish Clan & Family Encyclopedia*, pp. 278 - 279.
Zug, Marcia, "The Mail-Order Brides of Jamestown, Virginia," Aug 31, 2016, https://www.theatlantic.com/business/archive/2016/08/the-mail-order-brides-of-jamestown-virginia/498083/

Robert Coleman
Bellingham Castle, http://www.bellinghamcastle.ie/
Brenner, Robert: *Merchants and Revolution: Commercial Change, Political Conflict, and London's Overseas Traders*, London:Verso (2003)
"History of Lavenham Guildhall," National Trust.
Jones, Dan (2013). *The Plantagenets: The Warrior Kings and Queens Who Made England*. Viking.

"Kinderton Hall," https://historicengland.org.uk/listing/the-list/list-entry/1012358
Roper, Corinne. "Lavenham: The man-made wonder of Suffolk," BBC Suffolk.
Coleman, William Gilbert, "An Ancient & Worthy Family, 2015"; https://www.ancestry.com/mediaui-viewer/collection/1030/tree/36865069/person/19086774262/media/3c6074a4-e6a8-452d-8907-c72e118801c7?_phsrc=Prd3412&usePUBJs=true
Round, J. Horace (1901). *The Spencers and the Despencers, the Baronage*. The Baronage Press Ltd and Pegasus Associates Ltd. Retrieved 1 January 2017
Salzman, L.F. (ed), (1949), "Parishes: Wormleighton, A History of the County of Warwick," *Volume 5: Kington Hundred*, pp. 218–224.
"The Reign of Charlemagne," History Channel, http://www.history.com/topics/charlemagne
Riche, Pierre: *The Carolingians:The Family Who Forged Europe*. University of Pennsylvania Press (1983)

James Crews
"Baron Crew": https://en.wikipedia.org/wiki/Baron_Crew
Douglass, David: "James Crewes biography," https://www.wikitree.com/wiki/Crewes-3
Harbury, Katharine E.: "James Crewes (1622 or 1623–1677)," *Dictionary of Virginia Biography*
"Crews," Surname D B: http://www.surnamedb.com/Surname/Crewes#ixzz4enn-l4NSv
"Virginia Gleanings in England, Margaret Cruse of Essex and Virginia," *Virginia Magazine of History and Biography*, Volume XIII (July, 1905), No. 1, pages 53-64

Capt. Raleigh Croshaw
"Croshaw," Surname DB, http://www.surnamedb.com/Surname/Croshaw#ixzz4kSBxM3DQ
Hidden, Martha Woodroof: "Crowshaw," *William and Mary Qtrly (2), XXI,* pp265 70.
Raleigh Croshaw, Wikipedia, https://en.wikipedia.org/wiki/Raleigh_Croshaw
Raymond, Shirley, "Re: Captain Raleigh Croshaw," http://www.genealogy.com/forum/surnames/topics/croshaw/196/
Smith, John: *"General Historie, Vol III,* pp 78 81, Vol IV, pp. 151 154.

John Davis
Davis surname: https://en.wikipedia.org/wiki/Davis_(surname)
Davis/Davies Surname Genealogy: http://www.selectsurnamelist.com/davis.html
History of Isle of Wight County, http://www.iwchs.com/IWCHistory.html
O'Hart, John: *Irish pedigrees; or, The origin and stem of the Irish nation (1892), Vol 1 & 2*

John English
Caswell, Diana: "Early Watts Family Immigrants to Virginia," http://www.genealogy.com/forum/surnames/topics/watts/7005/
John Watts (Cherokee chief) https://en.wikipedia.org/wiki/John_Watts_(Cherokee_chief)
"Horsham: General history of the town," British History Online, http://www.british-history.ac.uk/vch/sussex/vol6/pt2/pp131-156

Elizabeth Gorsuch

Bennett Family History, "The Rev. John Gorsuch," https://www.facebook.com/pg/bennettgenealogy/photos/?tab=album&album_id=260294737452047

Forebears, "Gorsuch Surname Distribution," http://forebears.io/surnames/gorsuch

Harding, Samuel B.: *The Story of England*, "The Civil War Between King and Parliament (1642-1649)" http://www.mainlesson.com/display.php?author=harding&book=england&story=civil

Plesants, J. Hall: "The Gorsuch & Lovelace Families," published originally in *Virginia Magazine of History & Biography* and reprinted in Genealogies of Virginia Families (Balto. Gen Pub. Co. 1981) III, 242-443

Capt. Thomas Graves

"Beeley, Peak District Villlage Guides," http://www.peakdistrictonline.co.uk/beeley-c109.html

Burke's Commoners of Great Britain and Ireland, Provo, UT, USA: Ancestry.com Operations, Inc., 2002.

"Captaine Thomas Graves for Smythe's Hundred, The First Legislative Assembly, Historic Jamestowne," nps.gov

Records of the Virginia Company of London, vol. IV, p 364

Rixford, Elizabeth M. Leach: *Families Directly Descended from All the Royal Families of Europe (495-1932)*, "Graves Family," p. 57

Capt. Henry Isham

Ancestral Records and Portraits, Vol. 2, pp 751-752; Colonial Dames of America,, Baltimore, Grafton Press 1910

Bruce A. Bailey, "Isham, Sir Charles Edmund, tenth baronet (1819–1903)" *Oxford Dictionary of National Biography*, Oxford University Press, 2004

Hall, Sharon: "Digging History," http://digging-history.com/2014/03/15/surname-saturday-isham/

"Lamport Hall." Online reference http://www.kellner.eclipse.co.uk/northants/nlamport.htm

"Lamport Hall." Online reference https://en.wikipedia.org/wiki/Lamport_Hall

Williams and Martin, *The Domesday Book: A Complete Translation;* London: Penguin, 1992

William Leake

Bardsley, C.W., *A Dictionary of English and Welsh Surnames: With Special American Instances*. Wiltshire: Heraldry Today, 1901.

Chappelear, George W.: *Families of Virginia: The Leake Family and Connecting Lines*, The Shenandoah Press, Dayton, Virginia, 1932.

Tyler, Lyon Gardiner, editor, *Encyclopedia of Virginia Biography Vol. 4*, pp 105-106

Thomas Mask

Forebears, "Mask Surname Distribution," http://forebears.io/surnames/mask

Mask, Dalia Matos: "The Mask Family," http://deemask.tribalpages.com/

Surname DB, "Last Name: Maskew," http://www.surnamedb.com/Surname/Maskew#ixzz4wkflsrHt

Samuel Matthew

Chisholm, Hugh, ed. "Matthew, Tobias". Encyclopædia Britannica (11th ed.). Cambridge University Press. p. 896

Chalmers' General Biographical Dictionary, Vol. 21, pp 461-465, Provo, UT, USA: Ancestry.com Operations Inc, 2010.

Cooke, John Esten (1883), *Virginia: A History of the People,* Houghton, Mifflin and Co. p. 205.

Tyler, Lyon Gardiner, ed. *Encyclopedia of Virginia Biography. Volume 1.* New York, Lewis Historical Publishing Company, 1915, p. 148.

Bruce, Philip Alexander (1893). *The Virginia Magazine of History and Biography.* Virginia Historical Society. p. 91.

"Samuel Matthews": https://en.wikipedia.org/wiki/Samuel_Mathews

Helen Metland/Maitland

"Clan Maitland History," ScotClans, http://www.scotclans.com/scottish-clans/clan-maitland/maitland-history/

Dixon, Piers; Anderson, Iain; O'Grady, Oliver: "The Evolution of a Castle, Tibbers, Dumfriesshire: Measured and Geophysical Survey, 2013–14" (2015)

Hewison, J.K., Transaction, Volume 5, Glasgow Archaeological Society, pp. 150-151

Lennoxlove House or Lethington: http://portal.historicenvironment.scot/designation/LB10814

Richard New

Allgood, Ann Wall and Huff, Janet New: *The Family of New: Genealogy of Descendants of Richard New, Immigrant to Virginia in 1637 ...,* A.W. Allgood, 1981

Bardsley, C.W., *A Dictionary of English and Welsh Surnames: With Special American Instances.* Wiltshire: Heraldry Today, 1901.

Bruce, Philip Alexander, *Economic History of Virginia in the Seventeenth Century, Vol I,* McMillan Company, 1895 (located in William & Mary's Swem library)

Henning, William Waller: *Statutes at Large; Being a Collection of All the Laws of Virginia from the First Session of the Legislature in the Year 1619, Vol. 1,* p. 381.

Moraley, William and Klepp, Susan E.: *The Unfortunate: The Voyage and Adventures of William Moraley an Indentured Servant,* Google Books

Nugent, Nell Marion: *Cavaliers and Pioneers: Abstracts of Virginia Land Patents and Grants, 1623-1666, Volume 1* Genealogical Pub. Co., 1934, p. 83

William and Thomas Powell

"Ronald Rowe Powells Family Tree": http://www.genealogy.com/ftm/p/o/w/Ronald-R-Powell/WEBSITE-0001/UHP-0094.html

Rita-A-Fishman-AZ: http://www.genealogy.com/ftm/f/i/s/Rita-A-Fishman-AZ/WEBSITE-0001/UHP-0185.html

Meredith Clapper: "Notes for Thomas AP Howell (Powell)," ancestry.com

William Randolph

"Clifford Castle," http://www.castlewales.com/clifford.html

"County Kildare Federation of Local History Groups," kildarelocalhistory.ie

Cowden, Gerald S.: "The Randolphs of Turkey Island: a Prosopography of the First Three Generations, 1650–1800" (PhD diss., College of William and Mary, 1977), pp. 47-51

Daniels, Jonathan Worth: *The Randolphs of Virginia,* Doubleday (1972)
Doubleday, H. Arthur; Page, William, eds. "The Victoria History of the County of Essex." Westminster. p. 533 (1903)
"Earl of Arundel," https://en.wikipedia.org/wiki/Earl_of_Arundel
Emery, Anthony: *Greater Medieval Houses of England and Wales, 1300–1500, Volume I: Northern England,* Cambridge University Press (1996)
Goodall, John: *Warkworth Castle and Hermitage, London: English Heritage* (2006)
Historic England" "Appleby Castle"; National Heritage List for England.
Historic England: "Pickering Castle: 11th century motte and bailey castle and 13th century shell keep castle"; National Heritage List for England.
Historic England: "Scarborough Castle"; National Heritage List for England.
"History of Arundel Castle," www.arundelcastle.org.
"Hornby Castle, Hornby, North Yorkshire," British Listed Buildings.
Lewis, Samuel: *A Topographical Dictionary of England.* Institute of Historical Research, 1848.
Lindsay, J; et al. "Hedingham Castle official website," www.hedinghamcastle.co.uk.
"Middleham Castle," Heritage,http://www.english-heritage.org.uk/visit/places/middleham-castle/history/
Randolph, Robert Isham: *The Randolphs of Virginia: A Compilation of the Descendants of William Randolph of Turkey Island and His Wife Mary Isham Of Bermuda Hundred* (1936)
Richardson, Douglas: *Magna Carta Ancestry: A Study in Colonial and Medieval Families,* ed. Kimball G. Everingham. II (2nd ed.). Salt Lake City (2011)
"Scarborough Castle, North Yorkshire," The Heritage Trail.
"Skipton Castle, a complete medieval fortress," http://www.skiptoncastle.co.uk/
Turkey Island Mansion, http://henrico.us/assets/Turkey-Mansion-layout
"William de Vescy." *Dictionary of National Biography.* London: Smith, Elder & Co. 1885–1900.

Joseph and John "Rocky Creek" Watson
"Last Will & Testament of John Watson," ancestry.com
Coleman, William Gilbert (2015) "An Ancient and Worthy Family," ancestry.com
Clan/Family Histories—Watt/Watson: http://www.rampantscotland.com/clans/blclanwatt.htm
"Clan Watson History," Scot Clans, http://www.scotclans.com/scottish-clans/clan-watson/watson-history/
Watson, Walter A., *Notes on Southside Virginia,* p. 128: ancestry.com
Furtado, Peter; Geddes, Candida; Harris, Nathaniel; Harrison, Hazel; Pettit, Paul: *Guide to Castles in Britain. Details and description of Rockingham Castle.* Hamlyn–Ordnance Survey. p. 138 (1987)

The Webbs
Abigale Webb Shakespeare, Find A Grave, https://www.findagrave.com/cgi-bin/fg.cgi?page=gr&GRid=173379830
Gottsacker, Jerry, 2008, "The Webb Family," http://webb.skinnerwebb.com/index.html
Lees-Milne, James, "Arden Family," *18th Edition of Burke's Peerage/Burke's Landed Gentry, volume 1*
Rockingham Castle website: http://www.rockinghamcastle.com/

Shelby Crawford, Clifton: https://www.geni.com/people/Abigail-Shakespeare/6000000007356789724
"Walker Family Tree," https://www.ancestry.com/family-tree/tree/15313302/family?usePUBJs=true
"William Micajah Webb I," https://www.geni.com/people/William-Webb-I/6000000002135517427
Dargue, William: "Park Hall (Part One)—The Manor House," http://www.birminghamhistory.net/2014/05/02/park-hall-part-one/ 2014)

Refugees

German: Johan Jurg and Johan Michael Meisser
Boffo, Al: "The Meisser Family, Germany to New York to Pennsylvania to Ohio," from the book, *A Genealogy of the Meisser Family (Meiser, Miser, Mizar, Myser): from the Founding in America by Immigrant Ancestors to the Present Time,* Lloyd E Mizer, Meisser Genealogy Association printed by Forry and Haker, Lancaster, Pennsylvania (1966)
Fort Zeller, www.fortzeller.com
"From Schoharie to Tulpehocken; Berks History Center," http://www.berkshistory.org/multimedia/articles/the-palatine-migration-1723/
Harper, John W. and Martha B., "The Palatine Migration—1723"
Knittle, Walter A.: "The Early Eighteenth Century Palatine Emigration: A British Government Redemptioner Project to Manufacture Naval Stores." (Philadelphia: Dorrance, p. 272. (1937)
Meiser, Joseph A. Jr: "A Geneology of the Meisser Family, Johan Jurg Meisser, First Immigrant," page 5; https://archive.org/stream/AGenealogyOfMeisserFamily/A%20Genealogy%20of%20%20Meisser%20Family_djvu.txt
Meiser Surname, House of Names, https://www.houseofnames.com/meiser-family-crest
Otterness, Philip: *Becoming German: The 1709 Palatine Migration to New York.* Ithaca, NY: Cornell University Press (2004)
"The Palatine Migration": http://www.berkshistory.org/multimedia/articles/the-palatine-migration-1723
Paxton, James: *Joseph Brant and His World: 18th Century Mohawk Warrior and Statesman,* Lorimer Illustrated History
Statt, Daniel: *Foreigners and Englishmen: The Controversy over Immigration and Population, 1660-1760.* Newark (DE: University of Delaware Press, pp. 122-130 (1995)

Scot-Irish: Thomas Wallace
1860 Federal Census, White Oak Township, El Dorado County, California.
Ancestry.com: Bovell name meaning and history
"Battle of the Boyne," https://en.wikipedia.org/wiki/Battle_of_the_Boyne
Brown, D.E.: *The Marriages of Washington Co. Virginia, 1993*
El Dorado County, California, land records, book 56, filed 22 Apr 1901.
El Dorado County probate records, file no. 173.
El Dorado County Recorder's Office, Deed Book E, p. 487, dated March 1, 1860.
"Irish-Catholic Immigration to America," https://www.loc.gov/teachers/classroommaterials/presentationsandactivities/presentations/immigration/irish2.html

Letter from Wallace nephew Thomas A. Bussong, Jan. 1, 1941, shared by researcher Kriss Replogle
"The Potato Famine and Irish Immigration to America," Constitutional Rights Foundation, http://www.crf-usa.org/bill-of-rights-in-action/bria-26-2-the-potato-famine-and-irish-immigration-to-america.html
"Ulster Scots," https://en.wikipedia.org/wiki/Ulster_Scots_people
"William Wallace," https://en.wikipedia.org/wiki/William_Wallace

Huguenots: Peter Tuly and Anthony Toncray
Ancestry.com: Revolutionary War records
Ancestry.com: Upper Berry France Births, 1557-1907
Brock, Robert Alonzo, "Documents Chiefly Unpublished Relating to the Huguenot Emigration to Virginia and the Settlement of Manakin-Town, Virginia Historical Society, 1886," p. 8.
Buck, C.M, *Eighteenth Century Documents of the Nine Partners Patent, Dutchess County, New York*, William P. McDermott, Gateway Press, 1979
Buck, C. M., Dutchess County, NY Tax Lists, 1718-1787, Kinship, 1990
Bugg, J.L. Jr., "The French Huguenot Frontier Settlement of Manakin Town," Virginia Magazine of History and Biography, 61:4, October 1953, pp. 359-392
Carlo, P.W., "Huguenot Refugees in Colonial New York: Becoming American in the Hudson Valley"
"Connecticut Panhandle": Wikipedia: http://en.wikipedia.org/wiki/Connecticut_Panhandle
Dickerson, M.S., *Huguenot Lineage Research: A Bibliography Based on Migration Routes*,
Fernow, B., Vol. XV, State Archives, Vol. 1, Albany, N.Y., 1887
National Huguenot Society, Bloomington, Minnesota
Fontaine, John, on VirginiaPlaces.org.
German Palatines, Wikipedia, http://en.wikipedia.org/wiki/German_Palatines
Goodcell, Roscoe, "Our Early Years, Part 1, On Mother's Side," p. 4-5.
Hasbrouck, Frank, The History of Dutchess County, New York, S.A. Matthieu, Poughkeepsie, N.Y, 1919
"History of Wytheville," on file at County Clerks Office, Wytheville, Virginia
"Huguenot": Wikipedia online encyclopedia
Huguenot Society of South Carolina online ancestor listing
The Huguenot Society of the Founders of Manakin in the Colony of Virginia, online
Nevin, Alfred, *Encyclopedia of the Presbyterian Church in the United States of America*, Philadelphia, Pennsylvania,1884
"New Paltz, New York": Wikipedia online encyclopedia
Norton. A.T., "History of the Presbyterian Church in the state of Illinois," W.S Bryan, St. Louis, 1879, p. 599
Oblong Land Conservancy, http://www.pawling.org/Pages/PawlingNY_WebDocs/OLC
Pawlett, N.M.: "Albemarle County Roads 1725-1816," Virginia Highway & Transportation Research Council, Charlottesville, Virginia, 1981/2003
"Pedigree of Tankard of Whixley," http://www.rotherhamweb.co.uk/genealogy/tankard.htm
"Presbyterianism": Wikipedia online encyclopedia
"Protestant Reformation": Wikipedia online encyclopedia

"Sancerre": Wikipedia online encyclopedia
Smiles, Samuel: *The Huguenots in France: After the Revocation of the Edict of Nantes*, Harper & Brothers Publishers, 1874, New York, NY.
Smith, P.H., *General History of Duchess [sic] County from 1609-1876, Inclusive*, Pawling, N.Y., 1877
"The Story of Huguenot Street": http://www.huguenotstreet.org/about_us/about_huguenot_street.php
"Tancred of Hauteville" Wikipedia online encyclopedia
"Tancred, Prince of Galilee": Wikipedia, http://en.wikipedia.org/wiki/Tancred,_Prince_of_Galilee
Tancred of Sicily, http://www.answers.com/topic/tancred-of-sicily
Tuley, W.F., "The Tuley Family Memoir, an Historical, Biographical and Genealogical Story of the Tuleys and the Floyd Family Connection in Virginia, Kentucky and Indiana," New Albany, Indiana, 1906, p. 6
"Who Were the Huguenots?" The National Huguenot Society, http://www.huguenot.netnation.com/general/huguenot.htm
Wertenbaker, T.J., *The Planters of Colonial Virginia*, Princeton University Press, 1922, pp. 119, 204, and 206.
World names public profiler, http://worldnames.publicprofiler.org/Default.aspx

Quakers: Harlan, Buffington, Francis, Duck, Oborn and Cooke

Bacon, Margaret: *Mothers of Feminism: The Story of Quaker Women in America*. San Francisco: Harper & Row. p. 24 (1986)
BBC: "Religions—Christianity: Quakers": http://www.bbc.co.uk/religion/religions/christianity/subdivisions/quakers_1.shtml
Bremer, Francis J.; Webster, Tom, eds.: *Puritans and Puritanism in Europe and America: A Comprehensive Encyclopedia*. ABC-CLIO. p. xli. I (2006)
Draper Collection of Tennessee and Kings Mountain Papers at the University of Wisconsin
"Ezekiel Harlan Sr," Find-a-Grave, www.findagrave.com
"Ellis Harlan," Find a Grave: www.findagrave.com
"How A Sleepy Pennsylvania Town Grew Into America's Mushroom Capital," The Salt, NPR, http://www.npr.org/sections/thesalt/2012/10/12/162719130/how-a-sleepy-pennsylvania-town-grew-into-americas-mushroom-capital
Levy, Barry. *Quakers and the American Family*. p. 113.
World Council of Churches. "Friends (Quakers)." Church Families.
Yount, David: *How the Quakers invented America*. Rowman & Littlefield. p. 82 (2007)

California Swiss: Frank X. Walker

Caraccio, David: "Sacramento is fastest growing big city in California," *The Sacramento Bee*. The McClatchy Company.
Curtis's Top Fives: "Top 5 Words to Describe Switzerland"; https://curtywurty83.wordpress.com/2007/06/06/top-5-words-to-describe-switzerland/
Dillion, Richard: *Fool's Gold, the Decline and Fall of Captain John Sutter of California*. New York City: Coward-McCann (1967)
MySwissAlps.com: https://www.myswissalps.com/aboutswitzerland/culturehistory/historyswitzerland
Roberts, Mike, "The rise and fall of the Walker Ranch," Village Life/El Dorado Hills, 2009: http://www.villagelife.com/news/the-rise-and-fall-of-the-walker-ranch/d

Scott, Edward B., *The Saga of Lake Tahoe, Vol. 1*, Sierra-Tahoe Publishing Company, 1957, Lake Tahoe, California
Stammbuch von Uri, "Walker," microfische, Family History Center, LDS Church
"Three Words for Switzerland": https://holeinthedonut.com/2007/08/06/three-words-for-switzerland-and-photo-library-available/

Cherokees
"Amatoya Moytoy," https://www.werelate.org/wiki/Person:Amatoya_Moytoy_%284%29
"Beloved Woman of the Cherokee — Nancy Ward," Manataka American Indian Council, https://www.manataka.org
"A Brief History of the Trail of Tears," www.Cherokee.org, http://www.cherokee.org/About-The-Nation/History/Trail-of-Tears/A-Brief-History-of-the-Trail-of-Tears
Cave, Alfred: "Abuse of Power: Andrew Jackson and the Indian Removal Act of 1830." *The Historian*, Vol. 65, No. 6 (winter 2003), pp. 1330-1353, published by: Wiley: http://www.jstor.org/stable/24452618
"Cherokee Phoenix and Cherokee Indians," *New Georgia Enchclopedia*: Georgiaencyclopedia.org.
"Duncan O'Bryant: Pioneer Baptist Missionary to the Western Cherokees." (Biography) by Baptist History and Heritage; Free Online Library
"Elizabeth A. Sackler Center for Feminist Art: The Dinner Party: Heritage Floor: Nancy Ward," Brooklyn Museum.
French, Laurence: *Legislating Indian Country: Significant Milestones in Transforming Tribalism*. Peter Lang, 2007, p. 50.
Gardner, Robert Granville: "Cherokees and Baptists in Georgia," Georgia Baptist Historical Society (1989)
"History of the Cherokee Indians," http://thomaslegion.net/historyofthecherokeeindians.html "Indian removal 1814-1858," PBS Resource Bank: https://www.pbs.org/wgbh/aia/part4/4p2959.html
Inskeep, Steve: Jacksonland: *President Andrew Jackson, Cherokee Chief John Ross, and a Great American Land Grab*. New York: Penguin Press (2015)
"The James Scrolls," http://thejamesscrolls.blogspot.com/2009/03/indian-trail-from-amatoya-moytoy-to-my.html
King, Duane H., ed.: *The memoirs of Lt. Henry Timberlake: the story of a soldier, adventurer, and emissary to the Cherokees, 1756-1765*. Cherokee, N.C., Museum of the Cherokee Indian Press (2007)
Lewy, Guenter, "Were American Indians the Victims of Genocide?" *Commentary Magazine*, Sept. 1, 2004, https://www.commentarymagazine.com/articles/were-american-indians-the-victims-of-genocide/
Smith, David Ray, "Nancy Ward," *The Tennessee Encyclopedia of History and Culture*, 2010; http://tennesseeencyclopedia.net/entry.php?rec=1464
Sturgis, Amy H. Sturgis: *The Trail of Tears and Indian Removal*. Greenwood Publishing Group. 2007, pp. 119–. (2007)
"Trail of Tears," Native American History—HISTORY.com," http://www.history.com/topics/native-american-history/trail-of-tears